THE DAY OF THE LORD IS COMING!

The prophecies of the prophets of ISRAEL!

David Hocking

Published by HFT Publications
PO Box 3927   Tustin, CA 92781
Copyright 2013 by HFT Publications

Printed in the United States of America

ISBN 978-093949738-6

TABLE OF CONTENTS

INTRODUCTION

There is a day coming to planet earth that will make all previous days seem insignificant by comparison! It will not be a pleasant day; it is day filled with terror and panic such as the people of earth have never experienced!

Disasters have come to earth on many occasions and those who have been a part of them and have survived will find it hard to believe that a worst scenario is soon to come, the consequences of which have never been seen in previous history!

The Bible warns of this coming day in many passages of its pages. The Apostle Paul, who wrote 14 of the 27 books in the New Testament, wrote these words about this coming day of the Lord:

"But of the times and the seasons, brethren, ye have no need that I write unto you. For yourselves know perfectly that the day of the Lord so cometh as a thief in the night. For when they shall say 'Peace and safety' – then sudden destruction cometh upon them,

as travail upon a woman with child; and they shall not escape."
(I Thessalonians 5:1-3)

Some want to believe that he was referring to what happened in 70 AD when Rome destroyed Jerusalem and the Second Temple of the Jews. That was indeed a terrible day in human history, a day that Jesus predicted would come. But, a worst day was prophesied frequently by the Bible that would surprise the world and plunge it into an incredible chaos with millions losing their lives in the horrible disasters that are coming.

Perhaps you are among those who have questioned these prophecies and doubt seriously that such disasters will come to planet earth. Maybe you have thrown such thinking into a general category of "conspiracy theories" or some wild ravings of religious people who use such talk to convince people of their particular religious viewpoint.

Hollywood has frequently produced movies showing enormous disasters to hit planet earth. Perhaps, you say, these are just movies that have nothing to do with reality. But, many people, including some brilliant scientists, have already concluded that the planet is headed for disaster and serious trouble in the near future.

The Bible speaks of a coming day that is certainly longer than 24 hours in length. It appears that these prophecies speak of a period of time that could last for several years. The very term "DAY OF THE LORD" is found 25 times in the Bible and is not the only description used of a coming time of great disaster upon planet earth. Sometimes we read of this coming time as the "DAY OF GOD'S VENGEANCE" or the "DAY OF GOD'S WRATH." Is God really angry at the whole planet, and is He planning to bring a catastrophic judgment to end human history as we have known it?

There is a phrase used often in the Bible that frequently corresponds to this coming DAY OF THE LORD and it is the simple wording "IN THAT DAY."

Many scholars of past and present times have noticed that this catastrophic period of time is mentioned a great deal in the books of the Bible that we call "the prophets." Books like Isaiah, Jeremiah, Ezekiel, and Daniel – we call them "Major Prophets" because of their size and content. However, there is a group of books that some scholars call "Minor Prophets" or "The Twelve" that seem to be an integrated system and frequently speak of coming disaster.

It is important to recognize that these prophetic books speak of judgments and disasters that have already occurred in human history. There are nations, leaders, and events mentioned that we know existed long ago. However, within these historical events, we have many references that were not fulfilled at the time in past history that is presented, but rather project into a future time that has not as yet occurred on planet earth.

One such book is the prophetic book of JOEL – just three short chapters in English (four in Hebrew – same content), but powerful in their teaching about a coming DAY OF THE LORD!

Many of the references of these prophetic books are quoted in the last book of the New Testament – the Book of Revelation. Revelation speaks of coming disasters upon planet earth and quotes the former prophets who spoke so often about it.

Some Bible teachers believe that Revelation was written prior to 70 AD and that its disasters and terrible judgments on planet earth are referring to the Roman invasion of Israel. We would all be relieved to believe that this opinion is the truth, but history teaches clearly that the Book of Revelation was written by the Apostle John in 95 AD, some 25 years after the Roman destruction. It is also evident in reading the Book of Revelation carefully that the extent of the consequences of these disasters has never occurred as yet in human history! It appears that this coming DAY OF THE LORD in which the environment is destroyed and millions of people will lose their lives – is still in our future!

It is our sincere desire as we present the facts concerning this coming DAY OF THE LORD that you will find hope and comfort in the midst of what we are facing, and come to believe that not only are these events about to transpire on planet earth, but that there is an answer for all of us concerning how we can prepare for this coming disaster and escape this holocaust of terror about to take place!

The Bible warns that many people will be deceived into thinking that such judgment will never take place. The Bible even says that a period of time preceding these judgments will be described as *"peace and safety."*

Yes, judgment is coming, and the results will be far worse than anything human history has ever encountered previously!

Chapter 1
BIBLE FACTS

The Bible is, in fact, the most accurate account of ancient history! Its mention of people, prophets, kings, priests, events, and details of past empires is indeed amazing and irrefutable!

In trying to understand what is going to happen on planet earth when the "DAY OF THE LORD" begins, we take a moment to examine what the Biblical material reveals. It is indeed awesome!

The actual phrase "THE DAY OF THE LORD" appears 25 times in the Bible, four of which are found in the New Testament. The companion phrase "IN THAT DAY" appears 115 times (43 of those times in the Book of Isaiah alone!) with seven usages in the New Testament.

A DAY OF GENERAL DECEPTION

The facts of the Bible state continually that this coming "DAY OF THE LORD" will be characterized by widespread deception. All around the world, people will be deceived by what is taking place.

The main focus of this deception will be the call for *"peace and safety."* Violence will dominate the planet, and its people want assurances that security and personal safety for their families will be enforced. Talk of peace will center on the constant turmoil and violence that will increase in the Middle East as it has in the past.

In the Bible Book of Daniel, there is a "COVENANT OF PEACE" that will be enforced upon the people of Israel.
Daniel 9:24-27 speaks of a coming *"prince"* who will bring a "peace" to the Middle East and an opportunity for the Jewish people to have a "temple" and a restoration of "sacrifices" in the process of agreeing to this proposal.

Unfortunately, this coming prince will break his promises and will stop the sacrifices of a rebuilt temple, and bring a time of terror upon the Jewish people such as they have never known in the past.

According to Bible facts, it will be the leaders of Israel who will deceive the common people about "peace." Consider the following passages from the Bible:

Isaiah 9:16 – *"For the leaders of this people cause them to err; and they that are led of them are destroyed."*

Jeremiah 6:13-14 – *"For from the least of them even unto the greatest of them every one is given to covetousness; and from the prophet even unto the priest every one dealeth falsely. They have healed also the hurt of the daughter of My people slightly, saying, Peace, peace; when there is no peace."*

Jeremiah 8:10-11 – *"Therefore will I give their wives unto others, and their fields to them that shall inherit them: for every one from the least even unto the greatest is given to covetousness, from the prophet even unto the priest every one dealeth falsely. For they have healed the hurt of the daughter of My people slightly, saying, Peace, peace; when there is no peace."*

Jeremiah 23:1-2 – *"Woe be unto the pastors that destroy and scatter the sheep of My pasture! saith the LORD. Therefore thus saith the LORD God of Israel against the pastors that feed My people; Ye have scattered My flock, and driven them away, and have not visited them: behold, I will visit upon you the evil of your doings, saith the LORD."*

Ezekiel 13:10 – *"Because, even because they have seduced My people, saying, Peace; and there was no peace"*

Ezekiel 13:16 – *"To wit, the prophets of Israel which prophesy concerning Jerusalem, and which see visions of peace for her, and there is no peace, saith the Lord GOD."*

It is a day of <u>GROSS DARKNESS</u>!

Joel 2:2 – *"A day of darkness and of gloominess, a day of clouds and of thick darkness..."*

Amos 5:18-20 – *"Woe unto you that desire the <u>day of the LORD</u>! to what end is it for you? the <u>day of the LORD</u> is darkness, and not light. As if a man did* *flee from a lion, and a bear met him; or went into the house, and leaned his hand on the wall, and a serpent bit him. Shall not the <u>day of the LORD</u> be darkness, and not light? Even very dark, and no brightness in it?*

Zephaniah 1:15 – *"That day is a day of wrath, a day of trouble and distress, a day of wasteness and desolation, a day of darkness and gloominess, a day of clouds and thick darkness."*

It is a day of <u>GREAT DISTRESS</u>!

Joel 2:1-2 – *"Blow ye the trumpet in Zion, and sound an alarm in My holy mountain: let all the inhabitants of the land tremble: for the <u>day of the LORD</u> cometh, for it is nigh at hand; A day of darkness and of gloominess, a day of clouds and of thick darkness..."*

Zephaniah 1:17 – *"And I will bring distress upon men, that they shall walk like blind men, because they have sinned against the LORD..."*

Luke 21:25-26 – *"And there shall be signs in the sun, and in the moon, and in the stars; and upon the earth distress of nations, with perplexity; the sea and the waves roaring; Men's hearts failing them for fear, and for looking after those things which are coming on the earth: for the powers of heaven shall be shaken."*

It is a day of <u>GEOLOGICAL DISASTER!</u>

Revelation 6:12-17 – *"And I beheld when He had opened the sixth seal, and, lo, there was a great earthquake; and the sun became black as sackcloth of hair, and the moon became as blood; And the stars of heaven fell unto the earth, even as a fig tree casteth her untimely figs, when she is shaken of a mighty wind. And the heaven departed as a scroll when it is rolled together; and every mountain and island were moved out of their places. And the kings of the earth, and the great men, and the rich men, and the chief captains, and the mighty men, and every bondman, and every free man, hid themselves in the dens and in the rocks of the mountains; And said to the mountains and rocks, Fall on us, and hide us from the face of Him that sitteth on the throne, and from the* *wrath of the Lamb: For the great <u>day of His wrath</u> is come; and who shall be able to stand?"*

It is a day of <u>GLOBAL DESTRUCTION</u>!

Isaiah 13:6 – *"Howl ye; for the <u>day of the LORD</u> is at hand; it shall come as a destruction from the Almighty."*
Isaiah 13:13 – *"Therefore I will shake the heavens, and the earth shall remove out of her place, in the wrath of the LORD of hosts, and in the <u>day of His fierce anger</u>."*

Joel 1:15 – *"Alas for the day! For the <u>day of the LORD</u> is at hand, and as a destruction from the Almighty shall it come."*

I Thessalonians 5:2-3 – *"For yourselves know perfectly that the <u>day of the LORD</u> so cometh as a thief in the night. For when they shall say, Peace and safety; then sudden destruction cometh upon them as travail upon a woman with child; and they shall not escape."*

II Thessalonians 1:8-9 – *"In flaming fire taking vengeance on them that know not God, and that obey not the gospel of our Lord Jesus Christ; Who shall be punished with everlasting destruction from the presence of the Lord, and from the glory of His power."*

Revelation 16:18-21 – *"And there were voices, and thunders, and lightnings; and there was a great earthquake, such as was not since men were upon the earth, so mighty an earthquake, and so great. And the great city was divided into three parts, and the cities of the nations fell: and great Babylon came in remembrance before God, to give unto her the cup of the wine of the fierceness of His wrath. And every island fled away, and the mountains were not found. And there fell upon men a great hail out of heaven, every stone about the weight of a talent: and men blasphemed God because of the plague of the hail; for the plague thereof was exceeding great."*

It is a day of <u>GRUESOME DEATH</u>!

Revelation 6:8 – *"And I looked, and behold a pale horse: and his name that was on him was Death, and Hell (Hades) followed with him. And power was given unto them over the fourth part of the earth, to kill with sword, and with hunger, and with death, and with the beasts of the earth."*

Revelation 9:15-16 – *"And the four angels were loosed, which were prepared for an hour, and a day, and a month, and a year, for to slay the third part of men. And the number of the army of the horsemen were two hundred thousand thousand: and I heard the number of them."*

Revelation 13:7 – *"And it was given unto him to make war with the saints, and to overcome them: and power was given him over all kindreds, and tongues, and nations."*

Revelation 13:15 – *"And he had power to give life unto the image of the beast, that the image of the beast should both speak, and cause that as many as would not worship the image of the beast should be killed."*

It is a day of <u>GODLY DELIVERANCE</u>!

Joel 2:12-13 – *"Therefore also now, saith the LORD, turn ye even to Me with all your heart, and with fasting, and with weeping, and with mourning: And rend your heart, and not your garments, and turn unto the LORD your God: for He is gracious and merciful, slow to anger, and of great kindness, and repenteth Him of the evil."*

Joel 2:32 – *"And it shall come to pass, that whosoever shall call on the Name of the LORD shall be delivered: for in Mount Zion and in Jerusalem shall be deliverance, as the LORD hath said, and in the remnant whom the LORD shall call."*

Joel 3:16 – *"The LORD also shall roar out of Zion, and utter His voice from Jerusalem; and the heavens and the earth shall shake: but the LORD will be the hope of His people, and the strength of the children of Israel."*

Again, the BIBLE FACTS about the coming DAY of the LORD include the following:

1. GENERAL <u>DECEPTION</u>
2. GROSS <u>DARKNESS</u>
3. GREAT <u>DISTRESS</u>
4. GEOLOGICAL <u>DISASTER</u>
5. GLOBAL <u>DESTRUCTION</u>
6. GRUESOME <u>DEATH</u>
7. GODLY <u>DELIVERANCE</u>

These, of course, are overall general descriptions of this coming DAY of the LORD.

Chapter 2
ARE YOU LISTENING?

One of the so-called "Minor Prophets" is the Book of Joel, 73 verses that speak powerfully about the coming DAY of the LORD.

Joel 1:1-7
"The word of the LORD that came to Joel the son of Pethuel. Hear this, ye old men, and give ear, all ye inhabitants of the land. Hath this been in your days, or even in the days of your fathers? Tell ye your children of it, and let your children tell their children, and their children another generation. That which the palmerworm hath left hath the locust eaten; and that which the locust hath left hath the cankerworm eaten; and that which the cankerworm hath left hath the caterpillar eaten. Awake, ye drunkards, and weep; and howl, all ye drinkers of wine, because of the new wine, for it is cut off from your mouth. For a nation is come up upon My land, strong, and without number, whose teeth are the teeth of a lion, and he hath the cheek teeth of a great lion. He hath laid My vine waste, and barked My fig tree: he hath made it clean bare,

and cast it away; the branches thereof are made white."

Undoubtedly as you have read the above words you have been confused and troubled by the graphic words and have wondered what in the world are these words saying? Join the club! Many people have stop reading the Book of Joel just because of these opening verses and how strange they sound to our modern ears.

WHO IS JOEL?

Let's start with the identity of this prophet named Joel. He is called *"the son of Pethuel."* However, we have no knowledge of the prophet or his family. Also, in this brief Book of Joel there is no mention of any king, and no mention of the northern kingdom of Israel that was destroyed in 722 BC by Assyria.

What we do know is that the Temple of Solomon is still standing (cf. Joel 1:14 and 2:17 – *"priests"*) and that Jerusalem has walls still standing (cf. Joel 2:7) which means that the destruction by Babylon in 586 BC has not as yet occurred.

IT IS THE WORD OF THE LORD!

The prophecy of this book begins simply and clearly by the words *"The word of the LORD that came to Joel, the son of Pethuel."* That powerful phrase (*"the word of the LORD"*) appears 258 times in the Bible (13 in the New Testament). The statement that says *"the word of the LORD came..."* is found 92 times, and when it says *"came unto me"* it appears in that form 46 times! The impact of this fact is presented often in the Hebrew prophets, including Jeremiah, Ezekiel, Hosea, Jonah, Micah, Zephaniah, Haggai, Zechariah, and Malachi – in addition to the Book of Joel.

You may not believe that there is a God Whose presence fills the universe, and Who created human life upon planet earth – that is certainly your right to do! However, make no mistake about what the Bible is saying – it clearly claims to be the direct revelation of the God of creation and all of life! The messages about the coming disasters to hit our planet are declared by the Hebrew prophets to be the direct communication of God Himself! We are reading, believe it or not, the very WORD of GOD!

WE ARE TO TELL OUR CHILDREN AND OUR GRANDCHILDREN AND ALL FUTURE GENERATIONS THAT THE DAY OF THE LORD IS COMING TO PLANET EARTH!

Joel 1:2-3 says it very clearly:

"Hear this, ye old men, and give ear, all ye inhabitants of the land. Hath this been in your days, or even in the days of your fathers? Tell ye your children of it, and let your children tell their children, and their children another generation."

Nothing like this message of Joel had ever been given before! All generations were to be told that the DAY OF THE LORD is coming to planet earth!

REMEMBER WHAT CERTAIN BUGS CAN DO TO YOUR CROPS!

Verse 4 is speaking about the devastation that these bugs can bring to agriculture. The bugs (flying insects) are illustrations of what invading armies can cause to farming and the basic needs of people.

Four kinds of bugs are mentioned: palmerworm, locust, cankerworm, and caterpillar.

Some believe that the most plausible argument about verse 4 is that these four Hebrew words are describing the various kinds of locusts. It reveals how they do their devastating work. (There are actually 10 different Hebrew words that describe the work of locusts.)

gazam – probably refers to the swarm of locusts as they first attack the fields.

arbeh – might refer to the power of these locusts.

yeleq – most believe that these are "young locusts" with lots of energy and intense appetites, making them extremely dangerous.

hash' - this might be a general term for "other locusts" since there are usually different kinds that will be a part of the attack.

Bible prophecy teachers have often connected Joel 1:4 with Revelation 9:3 when the *"bottomless pit"* (the abyss) *is* opened. Verse 3 says: *"And there came out of the smoke locusts upon the earth: and unto them was given power, as the scorpions of the earth have power."*

Interestingly, these *"locusts"* have a *"king"* over them who is *"the angel of the bottomless pit"* who is called by the Hebrew word *"Abaddon"* and the Greek word *"Apollyon."* The words mean "destroyer" and are clear references to the Devil or Satan.

Joel 1:5 points to the distress and disappointment which people will experience by this coming devastation: *"Awake, ye drunkards, and weep; and howl, all ye drinkers of wine, because of the new wine, for it is cut off from your mouth."*

The description of *"drunkards"* points to people guilty of self-indulgence and unconcerned about the things of the Lord and His Word. This locust plague is a "wake-up call."

A STRONG NATION WILL ATTACK!

Joel 1:6-7

"For a nation is come up upon My land, strong, and without number, whose teeth are the teeth of a lion, and he hath the cheek teeth of a great lion. He hath laid My vine waste, and barked My fig tree: he hath made it clean bare, and cast it away; the branches thereof are made white."

Since Joel makes no reference to the northern kingdom of Israel, the *"nation"* he is describing is probably Babylon.

Notice that the text speaks of the land that is being attacked as *"MY land."* The land belongs to the LORD, and we must be talking about Israel. Israel is also called a *"vine"* and a *"fig tree."* The attack is so severe, the trees and vines have been stripped clean of their fruit.
The passage also refers to those being attacked as *"MY vine"* and *"MY fig tree."*

If this passage is referring to Babylon's attack in 586 BC when Jerusalem and the Temple of Solomon were destroyed, is this all that is meant by Joel's teaching?

The chapter seems to imply more than a past attack by Babylon upon the Nation of Israel. Verse 15 warns: *"for the day of the LORD is at hand."* And, chapter two begins with sounding the alarm of the trumpet (shofar) *"for the day of the LORD cometh, for it is nigh at hand."*

The central point of this first paragraph in Joel's book is that we need to pay serious attention to what is being said in this prophetic book. The words *"Hear this"* and *"give ear"* are saying to all of us "ARE YOU LISTENING?" These words were said to *"all ye inhabitants of the land."*

Chapter 3
CRY TO THE LORD!

JOEL 1:8-20

"Lament like a virgin girded with sackcloth for the husband of her youth. The meat offering and the drink offering is cut off from the house of the LORD; the priests, the LORD'S ministers, mourn. The field is wasted, the land mourneth; for the corn is wasted: the new wine is dried up, the oil languisheth. Be ye ashamed, O ye husbandmen; howl, O ye vinedressers, for the wheat and for the barley; because the harvest of the field is perished. The vine is dried up, and the fig tree languisheth; the pomegranate tree, the palm tree also, and the apple tree, even all the trees of the field, are withered: because joy is withered away from the sons of men. Gird yourselves, and lament, ye priests: howl, ye ministers of the altar: come, lie all night in sackcloth, ye ministers of my God: for the meat offering and the drink offering is withholden from the house of your God.

Sanctify ye a fast, call a solemn assembly, gather the elders and all the inhabitants of the land into the house of the LORD your God, and cry unto the LORD, Alas for the day! For the day of the LORD is at hand and as destruction from the Almighty shall it come. Is not the meat cut off before our eyes, yea, joy and gladness from the house of our God? The seed is rotten under their clods, the garners are laid desolate, the barns are broken down; for the corn is withered. How do the beasts groan! the herds of cattle are perplexed, because they have no pasture; yea, the flocks of sheep are made desolate. O LORD, to thee will I cry: for the fire hath devoured the pastures of the wilderness, and the flame hath burned all the trees of the field. The beasts of the field cry also unto thee: for the rivers of waters are dried up, and the fire hath devoured the pastures of the wilderness."

The <u>REACTIONS</u> God wants from His people – Joel 1:8-13

Verses 8-9 describe a wedding where the bride is *"girded with sackcloth."* We are then told that the common offerings of worship have been *"cut off from the house of the LORD"* and the priests are mourning.

Verses 10-12 reveal that the *"harvest of the field is perished"* and the *"vine is dried up"* and *"all the trees of the field are withered."* The reason? *"because joy is withered away from the sons of men."*

Verse 13 then tells the priests to *"lament"* and to *"howl"* and to *"lie all night in sackcloth."* This is a call to repentance! Verse 14 calls for a *"fast"* and that what God wants is to *"cry unto the LORD."*

The response to this disastrous locust plague brings before us the question of God's involvement and our responsibility to the disasters that come in life. Believers seem to handle tragedies and disasters in different ways. For the prophet Joel, the locust plague is an act of God.

HOW WE LOOK AT DISASTERS!

1. Some believe that it proves God is not involved in the circumstances of life, including the weather!

If God has the power to stop it and does not do it, He is seen as cruel, lacking in compassion; If He does care, but cannot do anything about it, then He is weak, and not powerful like the Bible describes Him to be.

2. Some believe that disasters are the work of Satan and that God allows them to exist as a part of what the Bible describes as "spiritual warfare."

3. Some believe that these disasters are the result of sin in the lives of God's people.

4. Some believe that God is the cause behind the disasters for reasons and purposes that we cannot understand at the moment.

Psalm 148:8 says: *"Fire, and hail; snow, and vapors; stormy wind fulfilling His Word."*

The prophet saw this disaster of the locust plague as a judgment of God and a warning from God of future disaster. The proper response is to repent of our sinful attitudes and actions, and to trust God to fulfill His purposes in this world!

Isaiah 45:7 – *"I form the light, and create darkness: I made peace, and create evil (calamity; disaster): I the LORD do all these things."*

Isaiah 46:9-11 – *"Remember the former things of old: for I am God, and there is none like Me, declaring the end from the beginning, and from ancient times the things that are not yet done, saying, My counsel shall stand, and I will do all My pleasure; Calling a ravenous bird from the east, the man that executeth My counsel from a far country: yea, I have spoken it, I will also bring it to pass; I have purposed it, I will also do it."*

The <u>REASON</u> behind this plea for repentance – Joel 1:15-20

"Alas for the day! For the day of the LORD is at hand, and as a destruction from the Almighty shall it come. Is not the meat cut off before our eyes, yea, joy and gladness from the house of our God? The seed is rotten under their clods, the garners are laid desolate, the barns are broken down; for the corn is

withered. How do the beasts groan! The herds of cattle are perplexed, because they have no pasture; yea, the flocks of sheep are made desolate. O LORD, to Thee will I cry: for the fire hath devoured the pastures of the wilderness, and the flame hath burned all the trees of the field. The beasts of the field cry also unto thee: for the rivers of waters are dried up, and the fire hath devoured the pastures of the wilderness."

It is the coming of the DAY of the LORD that is used to motivate God's people to repent of their sin and turn to the LORD before it is too late! The text of verse 15 says *"as a destruction from the Almighty shall it come."*

Yes, the coming of the DAY of the LORD is a judgment of God upon planet earth!

Zephaniah 1:14-18 is describing the coming DAY of the LORD as though it were a future period of time that will come to planet earth, and it will be a day of *"darkness"* and *"destruction"* as well as unusual events in the heavens!

The results will include the removal of their joy (v. 16), the rottenness of their crops (v. 17), and the confused reactions of their animals (v. 18).

In verse 19, God's judgment is described as *"fire"* and a *"flame."* Verse 20 says that *"the fire hath devoured the pastures of the wilderness."* God's judgment is designed to lead all of His creation to cry unto Him alone for help!

Chapter 4
BLOW THE TRUMPET!

Joel 2:1-17

"Blow ye the trumpet in Zion, and sound an alarm in My holy mountain: let all the inhabitants of the land tremble: for the day of the LORD cometh, for it is nigh at hand; A day of darkness and of gloominess, a day of clouds and of thick darkness, as the morning spread upon the mountains: a great people and a strong; there hath not been ever the like, neither shall be any more after it, even to the years of many generations. A fire devoureth before them; and behind them a flame burneth: the land is as the garden of Eden before them, and behind them a desolate wilderness; yea, and nothing shall escape them. The appearance of them is as the appearance of horses; and as horsemen, so shall they run. Like the noise of chariots on the tops of mountains shall they leap, like the noise of a flame of fire that devoureth the

stubble, as a strong people set in battle array. Before their face the people shall be much pained: all faces shall gather blackness. They shall run like mighty men; they shall climb the wall like men of war; and they shall march every one on his ways, and they shall not break their ranks: Neither shall one thrust another; they shall walk every one in his path: and when they fall upon the sword, they shall not be wounded. They shall run to and fro in the city; they shall run upon the wall, they shall climb up upon the houses; they shall enter in at the windows like a thief. The earth shall quake before them; the heavens shall tremble: the sun and the moon shall be dark, and the stars shall withdraw their shining: And the LORD shall utter His voice before His army: for His camp is very great: for He is strong that executeth His word: for the day of the LORD is great and very terrible; and who can abide it?

Therefore also now, saith the LORD, turn ye even to Me with all your heart, and with fasting, and with weeping, and with mourning: And rend your heart, and not your garments, and turn unto the LORD your God: for He is gracious and merciful, slow to anger, and of great kindness, and repenteth Him of the evil. Who knoweth if He will return and repent, and leave a blessing behind Him; even a meat offering and a drink offering unto the LORD your God? Blow the trumpet in Zion, sanctify a fast, call a solemn assembly: Gather the people, sanctify the congregation, assemble the elders, gather the children, and those that suck the breasts: let the bridegroom go forth of his chamber, and the bride out of her closet. Let the priests, the ministers of the LORD, weep between the porch and the altar, and let them say, Spare thy people, O LORD, and give not Thine heritage to reproach, that the heathen should rule over them: wherefore should they say among the people, Where is their God?"

A WORD ABOUT THE TRUMPET

The word *"trumpet"* is found 61 times in the King James Version of the Bible, and the simple word *"trump"* twice (I Corinthians 15:52 and I Thessalonians 4:16). The Hebrew word *"Shofar"* is used 72 times and refers to a ram's horn, was curved, and without decoration.

The *Shofar* was blown at the following times and occasions:

1. Mount Sinai – Exodus 19:16
2. Day of Atonement – Leviticus 25:9
3. Conquest of Jericho –Joshua 6:4-5
4. Victory of Gideon – Judges 7:19-22
5. Times of worship – Psalm 81:1-4

The *Shofar* was blown also to announce the coming of armies and judgment - Cf. Jeremiah 4:5; Zephaniah 1:16.

The <u>CHARACTER</u> of the coming Day of the Lord – Joel 2:1-11

1. A day of <u>DISTRESS</u> – v. 1
   "all the inhabitants of the land tremble"

Luke 21:25-26 – *"And there shall be signs in the sun, and in the moon, and in the stars; and upon the earth distress of nations, with perplexity; the sea and the waves roaring; Men's hearts failing them from fear, and for looking after those things which are coming on the earth: for the powers of heaven shall be shaken."*

    2. A day of <u>DARKNESS</u> – v. 2a
        "A day of darkness and of gloominess, a day of clouds and of thick darkness."

The word *"darkness"* is a common picture of impending judgment as is found in the following Scriptures:

Isaiah 5:30 – *"And in that day they shall roar against them like the roaring of the sea: and if one look unto the land, behold darkness and sorrow, and the light is darkened in the heavens thereof."*

Jeremiah 13:16 – *"Give glory to the LORD your God, before He cause darkness, and before your feet stumble upon the dark mountains, and, while ye look for light, He turn it into the shadow of death, and make it gross darkness."*

Amos 5:18 – *"Woe unto you that desire the day of the LORD! to what end is it for you?   the day of the LORD is darkness, and not light."*

Amos 5:20 – *"Shall not the day of the LORD be darkness, and not light? Even very dark, and no brightness in it?"*

Amos 8:9 – *"And it shall come to pass in that day, saith the Lord GOD, that I will cause the sun to go down at noon, and I will darken the earth in the clear day."*

Zephaniah 1:14-15 – *"The great day of the LORD is near, it is near, and hasteth greatly, even the voice of the day of the LORD: the mighty man shall cry there bitterly. That day is a day of wrath, a day of trouble and distress, a day of wasteness and desolation, a day of darkness and gloominess, a day of clouds and think darkness."*

3. A day of <u>DEMONISM</u> – v. 2b
   "a great people and a strong; there hath not been ever the like, neither shall be any more after it, even to the years of many generations."

The unusual way in which this fact is stated and its uniqueness in human history brings up the possibility that it is referring to what Revelation 9 speaks of – a demonic plague like the world has never encountered!

4. A day of <u>DEVOURING</u> – v. 3
    "A fire devoureth before them and behind them a flame burneth: the land is as the garden of Eden before them, and behind them a desolate wilderness; yea, and nothing shall escape them."

Joel 2:5 adds: *"like the noise of a flame of fire that devoureth the stubble, as a strong people set in battle array."*

5. A day of <u>DANGER</u> – vv. 4-9

    (1) Their <u>APPEARANCE</u> was frightening!

Joel 2:4 – *"The appearance of them is as the appearance of horses; and as horsemen, so shall they run."*

Joel 2:6 – *"Before their face the people shall be much pained: all faces shall gather blackness."* – the Jewish Targum says "all faces are covered with a coating of black like a pot."

Isaiah 13:6-8 – *"Howl ye; for the day of the LORD is at hand; it shall come as a destruction from the Almighty. Therefore shall all hands be faint, and every man's heart shall melt: And they shall be afraid: pangs and sorrows shall take hold of them; they shall be in pain as a woman that travaileth: they shall be amazed one at another; their faces shall be as flames."*

    (2)   Their <u>APPROACH</u> was deafening!

Joel 2:5 – *"Like the noise of chariots on the top of mountains shall they leap...as a strong people set in battle array."*

    (3)   Their <u>ANXIETY</u> was painful!

Joel 2:6 – *"the people shall be much pained..."*

Isaiah 13:8 – *"And they shall be afraid: pangs and sorrows shall take hold them; they shall be in pain as a woman that travaileth..."*

Jeremiah 4:31 – *"For I have heard a voice as of a woman in travail, and the anguish as of her that bringeth forth her first child..."*

Jeremiah 6:24 – *"...our hands wax feeble: anguish hath taken hold of us, and pain, as of a woman in travail."*

Jeremiah 13:21b – *"...shall not sorrows take thee, as a woman in travail?"*
Jeremiah 22:23 – *"...when pangs come upon thee, the pain as of a woman in travail."*

I Thessalonians 5:3 – *"For when they shall say, Peace and safety; then sudden destruction cometh upon them, as travail upon a woman with child; and they shall not escape."*

    (4)   Their <u>ABILITIES</u> were overwhelming!

Joel 2:7-9 – *"They shall run like mighty men; they shall climb the wall like men of war; and they shall march every one on his ways, and they shall not break their ranks: Neither shall one thrust another; they shall walk every way in his path: and when they fall upon the sword, they shall not be wounded. They shall run to and fro in the city; they shall run upon the wall; they shall climb up upon the houses; they shall enter in at the windows like a thief."*

The specific mention of the attack on the *"wall"* lends to the view that Jerusalem had not as yet been destroyed by Babylon.

(5)   A day of <u>DISASTER</u> – v. 10

"The earth shall quake before them; the heavens shall tremble; the sun and the moon shall be dark, and the stars shall withdraw their shining."

Isaiah 13:10 – *"For the stars of heaven and the constellations thereof shall not give their light: the sun shall be darkened in his going forth, and the moon shall not cause her light to shine."*

Isaiah 13:13 – *"Therefore I will shake the heavens, and the earth shall remove out of her place, in the wrath of the LORD of hosts, and in the day of His fierce anger."*

Matthew 24:29-30 – *"Immediately after the tribulation of those days shall the sun be darkened, and the moon shall not give her light, and the powers of the heavens shall be shaken: And then shall appear the sign of the Son of man in heaven: and then shall all the tribes of the earth mourn, and they shall see the Son of man coming in the clouds of heaven with power and great glory."*

(6)   A day of <u>DESTRUCTION</u> - v. 11

Joel 2:11 – *"And the LORD shall utter His voice before His army: for His camp is very great: for He is strong that executeth His word: for the day of the LORD is great and very terrible; and who can abide it?"*

The Bible is like a computer software system, interweaving the passages throughout its pages. The Day of the LORD and the statements regarding this future day are remarkable in the various quotations that a person finds in the New Testament.

The <u>CALL</u> for repentance
Joel 2:12-17

"Therefore also now, saith the LORD, turn ye even to Me with all your heart, and with fasting, and with weeping, and with mourning: And rend your heart, and not your garments, and turn unto the LORD your God: for He is gracious and merciful, slow to anger, and of great kindness, and repenteth Him of the evil. Who knoweth if he will return and repent, and leave a blessing behind him; even a meat offering and a drink offering unto the LORD your God?

Blow the trumpet in Zion, sanctify a fast, call a solemn assembly: Gather the people, sanctify the congregation, assemble the elders, gather the children, and those that suck the breasts: let the bridegroom go forth of his chamber, and the bride out of her closet. Let the priest, the ministers of the LORD, weep between the porch and the altar, and let them say, Spare Thy people, O LORD, and give not Thine heritage to reproach, that the heathen should rule over them: wherefore should they say among the people, Where is their God?"

Repentance is a consistent theme in the Bible. The Hebrew prophets continued to preach repentance to a rebellious and wicked people. It is a much needed cry today as well as in the past.

JOHN preached repentance!

Mark 1:2-4 -*"As it is written in the prophets (Isaiah 40:3), Behold, I send My messenger before thy face, which shall prepare thy way before thee. The voice of one crying in the wilderness, Prepare ye the way of the Lord, make His paths straight. John did baptize in the wilderness, and preach the baptism of <u>repentance</u> for the remission of sins."*

JESUS preached repentance!

Mark 1:14-15 - *"Now after that John was put in prison, Jesus came into Galilee, preaching the gospel of the kingdom of God, and saying, The time is fulfilled, and the kingdom of God is at hand: <u>repent</u> ye, and believe the gospel."*

Matthew 4:17 – *"From that time Jesus began to preach, and to say, <u>Repent</u>: for the kingdom of heaven is at hand."*

The DISCIPLES were told to preach repentance!

Luke 24:46-48: *"Thus it is written, and thus it behooved Christ to suffer, and to rise from the dead the third day: And that* repentance *and remission of sins should be preached in His Name among all nations, beginning at Jerusalem. And ye are witnesses of these things."*

PETER preached repentance!

Acts 2:38 – *"Then Peter said unto them,* Repent, *and be baptized every one of you in the Name of Jesus Christ for the remission of sins, and ye shall receive the gift of the Holy Ghost."*

Acts 3:19 – *"*Repent *ye therefore, and be converted, that your sins may be blotted out, when the times of refreshing shall come from the presence of the Lord."*

PAUL preached repentance!

II Corinthians 7:9-11 – *"Now I rejoice, not that ye were made sorry, but that ye sorrowed to* repentance: *for ye were* *made sorry after a godly manner, that ye might receive damage by us in nothing. For godly sorrow worketh <u>repentance</u> to salvation not to be repented of: but the sorrow of the world worketh death. For behold this selfsame thing, that ye sorrowed after a godly sort, what carefulness it wrought in you, yea, what clearing of yourselves, yea, what indignation, yea, what fear, yea, what vehement desire, yea, what zeal, yea, what revenge! In all things ye have approved yourselves to be clear in this matter."*

In the above verses, the Apostle Paul outlined the meaning of true godly repentance. It does not mean merely to be sorry for what you have said or done. It is characterized by seven things:

1. CAREFULNESS

The Greek word *spoude* is used 14 times in the New Testament and refers to the speed or eagerness with which a person responds when confronted.

2. CLEARING OF YOURSELVES

The Greek word *apologia* refers to a defense or apologetic – an apology rooted in the desire to be forgiven for what you have done – it is used 8 times.

3. INDIGNATION

The Greek word *aganaktesis* is only found here in the New Testament. Many believe that this word refers to the "pain" that a person feels because of what sin has caused.

4. FEAR

The Greek word *phobos* refers to an attitude toward God, and in particular, a fear of consequences.

5. VEHEMENT DESIRE

The Greek word *epipothesis* is found 4 times in the New Testament, all of them in this passage. It refers to the conviction which the Holy Spirit places upon your heart – a strong desire to respond.

6. ZEAL

The Greek word *zelos* is a very common word and refers to the effort and desire to stop the sinful behavior and live a godly life.

7. REVENGE

The Greek word *ekdikesis* is used 9 times in the New Testament and refers to judgment as a defense. This is a willing acceptance of the judgment of God and the consequences of disgrace, shame, humiliation, and loss, with no effort to justify, defend, or excuse the sinful behavior.

A SUMMARY OF GODLY REPENTANCE

1. You <u>RESPOND</u> as soon as possible to the situation!
2. You <u>REACT</u> with a sincere apology and seek forgiveness!
3. You <u>REALIZE</u> the pain you have caused to others!
4. You <u>REMEMBER</u> the consequences of continuing in this sin!
5. You <u>RECOGNIZE</u> that this is a priority!

6. You <u>RESOLVE</u> to settle this matter in whatever ways possible!
7. You <u>RESTORE</u> whatever is possible to settle the matter and to accept the consequences of sin!

II Timothy 2:24-26 – *"And the servant of the Lord must not strive; but be gentle unto all men, apt to teach, patient, In meekness instructing those that oppose themselves; if God peradventure will give them repentance to the acknowledging of the truth; And that they may recover themselves out of the snare of the devil, who are taken captive by him at his will."*

The CHURCHES were told to preach repentance!

Revelation 2:5 – *"Remember therefore from whence thou art fallen, and <u>repent</u>, and do the first works; or else I will come unto thee quickly, and will remove thy candlestick out of his place, except thou <u>repent</u>."*

Revelation 2:16 – *"<u>Repent</u>; or else I will come unto thee quickly, and will fight against them with the sword of My mouth."*

Revelation 3:3 – *"Remember therefore how thou hast received and heard, and hold fast, and <u>repent</u>."*

Revelation 3:19 – *"As many as I love, I rebuke and chasten: be zealous therefore, and <u>repent</u>."*

The PEOPLE in the tribulation in the future will NOT repent!

Revelation 9:20-21 – *"And the rest of the men which were not killed by these plagues, yet <u>repented</u> not of the works of their hands, that they should not worship devils, and idols of gold, and silver, and brass, and stone, and of wood: which neither can see, not hear, nor walk: Neither <u>repented</u> they of their murders, nor of their sorceries, nor of their fornication, nor of their thefts."*
Revelation 16:9 – *"And men were scorched with great heat, and blasphemed the Name of God, which hath power over these plagues: and they <u>repented</u> not to give Him glory."*

Revelation 16:11 – *"And blasphemed the God of heaven because of their pains* *and their sores, and <u>repented</u> not of their deeds.”*

The evidence is overwhelming – the call to repent is a theme throughout the Bible.

The CALL for repentance found in Joel 2:12-17 is clearly stated in Joel 2:12-13a!

“Therefore also now, saith the LORD, turn ye even to Me with all your heart, and with fasting, and with weeping, and with mourning. And rend your heart, and not your garments, and turn unto the LORD your God.”

It includes the following five characteristics:

(1)   A <u>CHANGED</u> heart – *“turn ye even to Me”*
(2)   A <u>COMMITTED</u> heart – *“even to Me with <u>ALL</u> your heart”*
(3)   A <u>CONTRITE</u> heart – *“with fasting”*

(4) A <u>CONCERNED</u> heart – *"with weeping and with mourning"*

(5) A <u>CAREFUL</u> heart – *"rend your heart, and not your garments"*

In addition to above responses, we need to <u>RECOGNIZE</u> the Lord's attributes that draw us to Him!

Joel 2:13b-14 – *"for He is gracious and merciful, slow to anger, and of great kindness, and repenteth Him of the evil. Who knoweth if he will return and repent, and leave a blessing behind him; even a meat offering and a drink offering unto the LORD your God?"*

(1) He is GRACIOUS – He gives us what we do not deserve!

(2) He is MERCIFUL – He cares about what we are feeling!

(3) He is SLOW TO ANGER – He is longsuffering toward us!

(4) He is OF GREAT KINDNESS – He treats us with loving concern!

(5) He REPENTETH HIM OF THE EVIL – He reconsiders the judgment that we deserve!

The immediate <u>REACTION</u> that is needed – Joel 2:15-16

"Blow the trumpet in Zion, sanctify a fast, call a solemn assembly: Gather the people, sanctify the congregation, assemble the elders, gather the children, and those that suck the breasts: let the bridegroom go forth of his chamber, and the bride out of her closet."

(1) <u>SOUND</u> the trumpet!

This is a call to repentance, and is based on a warning of coming danger!

(2) <u>SANCTIFY</u> a fast!

Spiritual preparation is necessary to experience the repentance that the LORD God of Israel desires from His people!

(3) <u>STOP</u> what you are doing!

When true godly repentance takes place, there is no desire to wait or to argue that you will respond in time – NO! The time to STOP the sinful behavior is NOW!

The basic REASONS behind this call to repent – Joel 2:17

"Let the priests, the ministers of the LORD, weep between the porch and the altar, and let them say, Spare Thy people, O LORD, and give not Thine heritage to reproach, that the heathen should rule over them: wherefore should thy say among the people, Where is their God?

    (1)   To avoid the <u>RULE</u> of the heathen!

    (2)   To avoid the <u>REPROACH</u> of the heathen!

    (3)   To avoid the <u>RIDICULE</u> of the heathen!

Chapter 5
WHAT WILL HAPPEN IF WE REPENT?

Many people wonder about this matter – WHAT HAPPENS IF WE REPENT? Will God change His mind about the future events He has prophesied will come?

II Chronicles 7:14 is a promise that if God's people will humble themselves, and pray, seek His face, and turn from their wicked ways – THEN – He will hear from heaven, forgive their sin, and heal their land!

1. God's <u>ATTITUDE</u> toward His land!

Joel 2:18
"Then will the LORD be <u>jealous</u> for His land, and pity His people.

<u>NOTE:</u> The Bible clearly presents the truth that God is a jealous God. The word is used 19 times in the Bible with only one usage in the New Testament.

      (1)   He alone is to be worshipped!

Exodus 20:5 – *"Thou shalt not bow down thyself to them (graven images and false gods), nor serve them: for I the LORD thy God am a <u>jealous</u> God, visiting the iniquity of the fathers upon the children unto the third and fourth generation of them that hate Me."*

Exodus 34:14 – *"For thou shalt worship no other god: for the LORD Whose Name is <u>Jealous,</u> is a <u>jealous</u> God."*

Deuteronomy 4:24-26 – *"For the LORD thy God is a consuming fire, even a <u>jealous</u> God. When thou shalt beget children, and children's children, and ye shall have remained long in the land, and shall corrupt yourselves, and make a graven image, or the likeness of any thing, and shall do evil in the sight of the LORD thy God, to provoke Him to anger: I call heaven and earth to witness against you this day, that ye shall soon utterly perish from off the land whereunto ye go over Jordan to possess it; ye shall not prolong your days upon it, but shall utterly be destroyed."*

Deuteronomy 5:9 – *"Thou shalt not bow down thyself unto them, nor serve* them: *for I the LORD thy God am a jealous God, visiting the iniquity of the fathers upon the children unto the third and fourth generation of them that hate Me."*

Deuteronomy 6:14-15 – *"Ye shall not go after other gods, of the gods of the people which are found about you; For the LORD thy God is a jealous God among you lest the anger of the LORD thy God be kindled against thee, and destroy thee from off the face of the earth."*

Joshua 24:19-20 – *"And Joshua said unto the people, Ye cannot serve the LORD: for He is an holy God; He is a jealous God; He will not forgive your transgressions nor your sins. If ye forsake the LORD, and serve strange gods, then He will turn and do you hurt, and consume you, after that He hath done you good."*

    (2)   He will have mercy on His people!

Ezekiel 39:25 – *"Therefore thus saith the LORD GOD; Now will I bring again the captivity of Jacob, and have mercy upon the whole house of Israel, and will be jealous for My holy Name."*

    (3)   He will take vengeance on His enemies!

Nahum 1:2 – *"God is jealous, and the LORD revengeth; the LORD revengeth, and is furious; the LORD will take vengeance on His adversaries, and He reserveth wrath for His enemies."*

    (4)   He will restore Jerusalem!

Zechariah 1:14-16 – *"So the angel that communed with me said unto me, Cry thou, saying, Thus saith the LORD of hosts; I am jealous for Jerusalem and for Zion with a great jealousy. And I am sore displeased with the heathen that are at ease: for I was but a little displeased, and they helped forward the affliction. Therefore thus saith the LORD; I am returned to Jerusalem with mercies: My house shall be built in it, saith the LORD of hosts, and a line shall be stretched forth upon Jerusalem."*

Zechariah 8:2 – *"Thus saith the LORD of hosts; I was jealous for Zion with great*

jealousy, and I was jealous for her with great fury."

2. His <u>ANSWER</u> to His people about the northern army

Beginning at Joel 2:19, God is the speaker, and that continues to the end of the Book.

Joel 2:19-20
"Yea, the LORD will answer and say unto His people, Behold, I will send you corn, and wine, and oil, and ye shall be satisfied therewith: and I will no more make you a reproach among the heathen. But I will remove far off from you the northern army, and will drive him into a land barren and desolate, with his face toward the east sea, and his hinder part toward the utmost sea, and his stink shall come up, and ill savor shall come up, because he hath done great things."

> (1) Their <u>RELIANCE</u> upon the LORD will bring complete satisfaction – v. 19a
> *"and ye shall be satisfied"*

(2) Their <u>REPROACH</u> among the nations will be taken away – v. 19b – *"I will no more make you a reproach among the heathen"*

(3) The <u>REMOVAL</u> of the northern army will be accomplished by the LORD – v. 20 – *"because He hath done great things"*

3. His <u>ABILITY</u> should eliminate all fear – vv. 21-22

"Fear not, O land; be glad and rejoice: for the LORD will do great things. Be not afraid, ye beasts of the field: for the pastures of the wilderness do spring, for the tree beareth her fruit, the fig tree and the vine do yield their strength."

Isaiah 41:10 – *"Fear thou not; for I am with thee: be not dismayed; for I am thy God: I will strengthen thee; yea, I will help thee; yea, I will uphold thee with the right hand of My righteousness."*

Isaiah 41:13-14 – *"For I the LORD thy God will hold thy right hand, saying unto thee, Fear not; I will help thee.*

Fear not, thou worm Jacob, and ye men of Israel; I will help thee, saith the LORD, and thy Redeemer, the Holy One of Israel."

Isaiah 43:1 – *"But now thus saith the LORD that created thee, O Jacob, and He that formed thee, O Israel, Fear not: for I have redeemed thee, I have called thee by thy name; thou art Mine."*

Isaiah 43:5 – *"Fear not: for I am with thee: I will bring thy seed from the east, and gather thee from the west."*

Isaiah 44:2 – *"Thus saith the LORD that made thee, and formed thee from the womb, which will help thee; Fear not, O Jacob, My servant; and thou, Jesurun, whom I have chosen."*

Isaiah 44:8 – *"Fear ye not, neither be afraid: have not I told thee from that time, and have declared it? ye are even My witnesses. Is there a God beside Me? Yea, there is no God; I know not any."*

NOTE: The word *"great"* is found 962 times in the English Bible (708 in the Old Testament and 254 in the New

Testament). The phrase *"great things"* is used 19 times in the Old Testament and 9 times in the New Testament.

The following things about the God Who does *"great things"* – the One Whose ability eliminates all fear!

(1) There is no one like Him!

II Samuel 7:21-22 – *"For Thy word's sake, and according to Thine own heart, hast Thou done all these great things, to make Thy servant know them. Wherefore Thou art great, O LORD God: for there is none like Thee, neither is there any God beside Thee, according to all that we have heard with our ears."*

Psalm 71:19 – *"Thy righteousness also, O God, is very high, Who hast done great things: O God, who is like unto thee!"*

(2) These things are
        "unsearchable" and
        "without number"

Job 5:9 – *"Which doeth great things and unsearchable; marvelous things without number."*

Job 9:10 – *"Which doeth great things past finding out; yea, and wonders without number."*

Job 37:5 – *"God thundereth marvelously with His voice; great things doeth He, which we cannot comprehend."*

Psalm 145:3 – *"Great is the LORD, and greatly to be praised; and His greatness is unsearchable."*

> (3) These things cause joy in the hearts of God's people!

Psalm 126:1-3 – *"When the LORD turned again the captivity of Zion, we were like them that dream. Then was our mouth filled with laughter, and our tongue with singing: then said they among the heathen, The LORD hath done great things for them. The LORD hath done great things for us; whereof we are glad."*

> (4) These things should cause us to praise and worship Him!

I Chronicles 16:25-31 – *"For great is the LORD, and greatly to be praised: He also is to be feared above all gods. For all the gods of the people are idols: but the LORD made the heavens. Glory and honor are in His presence; strength and gladness are in His place. Give unto the LORD the glory due unto His Name: bring an offering, and come before Him: worship the LORD in the beauty of holiness. Fear before Him, all the earth: the world also shall be stable, that it be not moved. Let the heavens be glad, and let the earth rejoice: and let men say among the nations, The LORD reigneth.*

Psalm 48:1-2 – *"Great is the LORD, and greatly to be praised in the city of our God, in the mountain of His holiness. Beautiful for situation, the joy of the whole earth, is mount Zion, on the sides of the north, the city of the great King."*

> (5) All these things show us that there is nothing that God cannot do!

I Chronicles 29:10-13 – *"Wherefore David blessed the LORD before all the congregation: and David said, Blessed be Thou, LORD God of Israel our Father, forever and ever. Thine, O*

LORD, is the greatness, and the power, and the glory, and the victory, and the majesty: for all that is in the heaven and in the earth is Thine; Thine is the kingdom, O LORD, and Thou art exalted as Head over all. Both riches and honor come of Thee, and Thou reignest over all; and in Thine hand is power and might; and in Thine hand it is to make great, and to give strength unto all. Now therefore, our God, we thank Thee, and praise Thy glorious Name."

4. His <u>APPEAL</u> to His people to rejoice!

Joel 2:23-25 – "Be glad then, ye children of Zion, and rejoice in the LORD your God: for He hath given you the former rain moderately, and He will cause to come down for you the rain in the first month. And the floors shall be full of wheat, and the vats shall overflow with wine and oil. And I will restore to you the years that the locust hath eaten, the cankerworm, and the caterpillar, and the palmerworm, My great army which I sent among you."

Psalm 149:2 – *"Let Israel rejoice in Him that made him: let the children of Zion be joyful in their King."*

Philippians 4:4 – *"Rejoice in the Lord always, and again I say – REJOICE!*

(1) He <u>REGULATES</u> the weather – v. 23 – *"He will cause to come down for you the rain"*

(2) He <u>REPLENISHES</u> with overflowing – v. 24

(3) He <u>RESTORES</u> what was taken away – v. 25

5. His <u>ADORATION</u> will come from His people – v. 26

"And ye shall eat in plenty, and be satisfied, and praise the Name of the LORD your God, that hath dealt wondrously with you: and My people shall never be ashamed."

6. His <u>AIM</u> will be accomplished – v. 27

"And ye shall know that I am in the midst of Israel, and that I am the LORD your God, and none else: and My people shall never be ashamed."

SUMMARY

How wonderful to read the words of Joel 2 that clearly reveal that the Lord will bring His blessing and restoration to those who repent and seek His face!

Two things stand up in our minds and hearts as we review carefully these words from the LORD Himself:

1. The <u>NATURE</u> of God Himself!
2. The <u>POWER</u> of God over all things!

It is because of Who He is, and what He can do that brings hope to our hearts – even when hopelessness and despair has overwhelmed our culture. If we repent, God is merciful and gracious, and will forgive us, and restore and heal our land!

Chapter 6
THE HOLY SPIRIT AND GOD'S DELIVERANCE

The final words of Joel 2:28-32 reveal how God is going to bring His amazing deliverance to His people in spite of the horrors of the coming Day of the Lord.

These five verses that are found at the end of chapter two of Joel in our English Bibles form a complete new chapter in the Hebrew Bible. In that Hebrew Bible, there are four chapters in Joel, and the third chapter is the one before us now.

JOEL 2:28-32
"And it shall come to pass afterward, that I will pour out My Spirit upon all flesh; and your sons and your daughters shall prophesy, your old men shall dream dreams, your young men shall see visions: And also upon the servants and upon the handmaids in those days will I pour out My Spirit. And I will shew wonders in the heavens and in the earth, blood, and fire, and pillars of smoke. The sun shall be turned into darkness, and the moon into blood, before the great and the

terrible day of the LORD come. And it shall come to pass, that whosoever shall call on the Name of the LORD shall be delivered: for in mount Zion and in Jerusalem shall be deliverance, as the LORD hath said, and in the remnant whom the LORD shall call."

1. The <u>MEANING</u> of this event vv. 28-29

<u>NOTE:</u> The words *"pour out"* in reference to God's Spirit are used in five places in the Old Testament, and only three places in the New Testament. We need to read these usages carefully.

Proverbs 1:23 – *"Turn you at My reproof: behold, I will pour out My Spirit unto you, I will make known My words unto you."*

Ezekiel 39:29 – *"Neither will I hide My face any more from them: for I have poured out My Spirit upon the house of Israel, saith the Lord GOD."*

Joel 2:28-29 – *"And it shall come to pass afterward, that I will pour out My Spirit upon all flesh; and your sons and your daughters shall prophesy, your old men shall dream dreams, your young men shall see visions: And also upon the servants and upon the handmaids in those days will I pour out My Spirit."*

Zechariah 12:10 – *"And I will pour out upon the house of David, and upon the inhabitants of Jerusalem, the Spirit of grace and of supplications: and they shall look upon Me Whom they have pierced, and they shall mourn for Him, as one mourneth for his only son, and shall be in bitterness for Him, as one that is in bitterness for His firstborn."*

Acts 1:17-18 – *"And it shall come to pass in the last days, saith God, I will pour out of My Spirit upon all flesh: and your sons and your daughters shall prophesy, and your young men shall see visions, and your old men shall dream dreams: And on My servants and on My handmaidens I will pour out in those days of My Spirit; and they shall prophesy."*

Acts 10:45 – *"And they of the circumcision which believed were astonished, as many as came with Peter, because that on the Gentiles also, was poured out the gift of the Holy Ghost."*

In Acts 11:15 when Peter recounts what happened when the Holy Spirit was poured out upon the Gentiles, he says: *"the Holy Ghost fell on them, as on us at the beginning."*

In Acts 11:17, Peter makes it clear that this happened because they *"believed on the Lord Jesus Christ."* The response of the leaders in Jerusalem was (Acts 11:18): *"Then hath God also to the Gentiles granted repentance unto life."*

WHAT WAS THE MEANING OF THE POURING OUT OF THE HOLY SPIRIT?

1. It refers to the <u>PRESENCE</u> of the Holy Spirit in the lives of all believers!

2. It refers to the <u>POWER</u> of the Holy Spirit in giving the believers boldness to witness and control over sinful attitudes and actions!

The <u>MULTITUDE</u> who received the Holy Spirit

Acts 2:38-42 – *"Then Peter said unto them, Repent, and be baptized every one of you in the Name of Jesus Christ for the remission of sins, and ye shall receive the gift of the Holy Ghost. For the promise is unto you, and to your children, and to all that are afar off, even as many as the Lord our God shall call. And with many other words did he testify and exhort, saying, Save yourselves from this untoward generation. Then they that gladly received his word were baptized: and the same day there were added unto them about three thousand souls. And they continued stedfastly in the apostles' doctrine and fellowship, and in breaking of bread, and in prayers."*

The Bible teaches that the multitude who received the Holy Spirit were described as:

> *"all flesh"*
> *"sons and daughters"*
> *"old men and young men"*
> *"servants and handmaidens"*

The **MARVELS** that will occur in the heavens and on the earth!

1. **DESTRUCTION** on the earth
   "blood, and fire, and pillars of smoke"

2. **DARKNESS** in the sky
   "the sun shall be turned into darkness, and the moon into blood"

3. **DISASTER** in stellar space
   "the stars shall fall from heaven, and the powers of the heavens shall be shaken"

4. **DISTRESS** among the nations
   "and upon the earth distress of nations, with perplexity; the sea and the waves roaring; men's hearts failing them for fear."

The **MIRACLE** of deliverance
"whosoever shall call on the Name of the LORD shall be delivered"

The **MOUNT** where this will take place – *"for in Mount Zion and in Jerusalem shall be deliverance"*

The words *"Mount Zion"* are used 18 times in Bible – 5 in the Psalms, and 13 in Isaiah.

WHAT DO THE WORDS *"MOUNT ZION"* MEAN?

1. It is the joy of the whole world!

Psalm 48:1-2 – *"Great is the LORD, and greatly to be praised in the city of our God, in the mountain of His holiness. Beautiful for situation, the joy of the whole earth, is mount Zion, on the sides of the north, the city of the great King."*

2. It is where God dwells!

Psalm 74:2 – *"Remember Thy congregation, which Thou hast purchased of old; the rod of Thine inheritance, which Thou hast redeemed; this mount Zion, wherein Thou hast dwelt."*

Isaiah 8:18 – *"Behold, I and the children whom the LORD hath give me are for signs and for wonders in Israel from the LORD of hosts, which dwelleth in mount Zion."*

3. It is the place God loves!

Psalm 78:68 – *"But chose the tribe of Judah, the mount Zion which he loved."*

4. It will abide forever!

Psalm 125:1 – *"They that trust in the LORD shall be as mount Zion, which cannot be removed, but abideth forever."*

5. It will be defended by God!

Isaiah 4:5-6 – *"And the LORD will create upon every dwelling place of mount Zion, and upon her assemblies, a cloud and smoke by day, and the shining of a flaming fire by night: for upon all the glory shall be a defense. And there shall be a tabernacle for a shadow in the daytime from the heart, and for a place of refuge, and for a covert from storm and from rain."*

6. It will be the place where the Messiah will reign!

Isaiah 24:23 – *"Then the moon shall be confounded, and the sun ashamed, when the LORD of hosts shall reign in mount Zion, and in Jerusalem, and before His ancients gloriously."*

Micah 4:7 – *"And I will make her that halted a remnant, and her that was cast far off a strong nation: and the LORD shall reign over them in mount Zion from henceforth, even forever."*

7. It is the place over which the Messiah will fight!

Isaiah 31:4 – *"For thus hath the LORD spoken unto me, Like as the lion and the young lion roaring on his prey, when a multitude of shepherds is called forth against him, he will not be afraid of their voice, nor abase himself for the noise of them: so shall the LORD of hosts come down to fight for mount Zion, and for the hill thereof."*

8. It is the place of deliverance!

Obadiah 17 – *"But upon mount Zion shall be deliverance, and there shall be holiness; and the house of Jacob shall possess their possessions."*

The <u>MOMENT</u> that this will occur!

Joel 2: 28 – *"And it shall come to pass afterward..."*

Joel 2:32 – *"And it shall come to pass..."*

Joel 2:31 – *"before the great and the terrible day of the LORD come."*

Joel 3:14 – *"Multitudes, multitudes in the valley of decision; for the day of the LORD is near in the valley of decision."*

Zephaniah 1:14-17 – *"The great day of the LORD is near, it is near, and hasteth greatly, even the voice of the day of the LORD: the mighty man shall cry there bitterly. That day is a day of wrath, a day of trouble and distress, a day of wasteness and desolation, a day of darkness and gloominess, a day of clouds and thick darkness, a day of the trumpet and alarm against the fenced cities, and against the high towers."*

I Timothy 4:1 – *"Now the Spirit speaketh expressly, that in the latter times some shall depart from the faith, giving heed to seducing spirits and doctrines of devils."*

II Timothy 3:1 – *"This know also, that in the last days perilous times shall come."*

II Peter 3:3-4 – *"Knowing this first, that there shall come in the last days scoffers, walking after their own lusts, and saying, Where is the promise of His coming? For since the father fell asleep, all things continue as they were from the beginning of creation."*

II Peter 3:10 – *But the day of the Lord will come as a thief in the night; in the which the heavens shall pass away with a great noise, and the elements shall melt with fervent heat, the earth also and the works that are therein shall be burned up."*

The emphasis on the timing of these disasters centers in the phrase used 25 times in the Bible – THE DAY OF THE LORD!

Chapter 7
VALLEY OF DECISION

Joel 3:1-21 is chapter 4 in the Hebrew Bible but contains the same content.
It presents details about the coming Day of the LORD which are not found in other passages.

1. The <u>RETURN</u> of the Jewish people will mark the time!

Joel 3:1 – *"For, behold, in those days, and in that time, when I shall bring again the captivity of Judah and Jerusalem."*

<u>NOTE</u>: It appears from the Biblical evidence that there will be two returns of Jewish people to their promised land.
One involves the return of Jewish people to the Land in unbelief. It appears that this is the Aliyah (return) that is occurring today.

There are currently Jewish people from 185 countries of the world who are now full Israeli citizens and living in the Land of Israel. These are the Jewish people who will be redeemed by the coming of the Messiah for they will *"look on Him Whom they have pierced."*

However, it also seems clear that a Jewish return will happen again, and this time it will be believers. Joel 3:1 quotes the LORD Himself Who says *"when I shall bring <u>AGAIN</u> the captivity of Judah and Jerusalem."*

Isaiah 11:11 also says: *"And it shall come to pass in that day, that the Lord shall set His hand <u>AGAIN</u> the <u>second time</u> to recover the remnant of His people."*

2. The <u>REASONS</u> behind the coming judgment of God upon all nations!

Joel 3:2-3 — *"I will also gather all nations, and will bring them down into the valley of Jehoshaphat, and will plead with them there for My people and for My heritage Israel, whom they have scattered among the nations, and parted My land. And they have cast lots for My people; and have given a boy for an harlot, and sold a girl for wine, that they might drink."*

The LORD will *"gather ALL nations"* in this valley of decision. The word *"Jehoshaphat"* means "Yahveh judges."

    (1)   The <u>SCATTERING</u> of God's people – *"whom they have scattered among the nations"*

    (2)   The <u>SPLITTING</u> of the Land *"and parted My land."*

<u>NOTE:</u> Ever since the so-called "peace process" between Israel and the Palestinian Arabs was announced on September 13, 1993, the world seems bent on taking land away from Israel. The world keeps saying that it is "occupied land" and implies that Israel has taken it away from Palestinians who supposedly owned the land previously. That is a bold face LIE!

Daniel 11:39 speaks of the coming actions of a world leader who will seek to *"divide the land for gain."*

    (3)   The <u>SELLING</u> of children for immorality – v. 3

Amos 2:6 says: *"Thus saith the LORD; For three transgressions of Israel, and for four, I will not turn away the punishment thereof; because they sold the righteous for silver, and the poor for a pair of shoes."*

The price of these slaves only bought a night with a prostitute or a little wine – it reveals how cheaply they were regarded.

Exodus 21:16 says: *"And he that stealeth a man, and selleth him, or if he be found in his hand, he shall surely be put to death."*

The <u>RECOMPENSE</u> of God will come to the nations!

Joel 3:4-8 – *"Yea, and what have ye to do with Me, O Tyre, and Zidon, and all the coasts of Palestine? Will ye render Me a recompense? And if ye recompense Me, swiftly and speedily will I return your recompence upon your own head; Because ye have taken My silver and My gold, and have carried into your temples My goodly pleasant things: The children also of Judah and the children of Jerusalem have ye sold unto the Grecians, that ye might remove them far from their border. Behold, I will raise them out of the place whither ye have sold them, and will return your recompence upon your own head: And I will sell your sons and your daughters into the hand of the children of Judah, and they shall sell them to the Sabeans, to a people far off: for the LORD hath spoken it."*

    (1)   He <u>**CONFRONTS**</u> Lebanon and the Palestinians – v. 4

"Yea, and what have ye to do with Me, O Tyre, and Zidon, and all the coasts of Palestine?"

    (2)   He <u>**CONDEMNS**</u> them for robbing His people – v. 5

"Because ye have taken My silver and My gold, and have carried into your temples My goodly pleasant things."

    (3)   He <u>**CORRECTS**</u> their selling of Jewish captives – vv. 6-8a

"Behold, I will raise them out of the place whither ye have sold them..."

(4)   He **CONFIRMS** that all this will take place because it is His Word! v. 8b – *"for the LORD hath spoken it"*

The **ROUSING** of the nations to battle will be accomplished by the Lord Himself!

Joel 3:9-12
"Proclaim ye this among the Gentiles; Prepare war, wake up the mighty men, let all the men of war draw near; let them come up: Beat your plowshares into swords, and your pruninghooks into spears; let the weak say, I am strong. Assemble yourselves, and come, all ye heathen, and gather yourselves together round about: thither cause thy mighty ones to come down, O LORD. Let the heathen be wakened, and come up to the valley of Jehoshaphat: for there will I sit to judge all the heathen round about."

THE COMING DAY OF THE LORD WILL BRING ALL NATIONS AND THEIR ARMIES TO ISRAEL WHERE THE LORD GOD OF ISRAEL WILL JUDGE THEM!

(1)   The <u>INVITATION</u> is to <u>ALL</u>
        nations! v. 11a

"Come, all ye heathen (nations) *and
gather yourselves together."*

The Hebrew word *goyim* is translated as
"Gentiles" or "heathen" or "nations."

(2)   The   <u>INVOLVEMENT</u>   of
        angels in this judgment – v.
        11b

*"cause Thy mighty ones to come down,
O LORD."*

The Bible speaks of the judgment of
angels in I Corinthians 6:3: *"Know ye
not that we shall judge angels? How
much more things that pertain to this
life?"*

II Peter 2:4 says: *"For if God spared not
the angels that sinned, but cast them
down to hell* (Tartaros), *and delivered
them into chains of darkness, to be
reserved unto judgment."*

Some believe that this is simply a call for
God's good and mighty angels to be
involved   in   the   conflict   that   will

conclude the tribulation period; However, the Messiah will NOT need the help of the angels in this final conflict. According to Isaiah 63 He will handle it all by Himself!

There is a New Testament reference to the good angels being involved at the end of the tribulation or the Day of the LORD. We read the following in Matthew 13:41-42

"The Son of man shall send forth His angels, and they gather out of His kingdom all things that offend, and them which do iniquity; and shall cast them into a furnace of fire: there shall be wailing and gnashing of teeth."

We also read in Matthew 25:31-32 these important words:

"When the Son of man shall come in His glory, and all the holy angels with Him, then shall He sit upon the throne of His glory: And before Him shall be gathered all nations: and He shall separate them one from another, as a shepherd divideth his sheep from the goats."

WHAT JUDGMENTS ARE HANDLED BY GOD AND HIS SON, JESUS CHRIST OUR LORD?

JUDGMENT OF BELIEVERS IN THIS LIFE

> Attitudes about the Bread & Cup
> I Corinthians 11:27-32
>
> Actions that deal with our faults
> I Peter 2:17-20
>
> Attacks that bring glory to God
> I Peter 4:12-19

JUDGMENT SEAT OF CHRIST (believers only)

Romans 14:10-13; I Corinthians 3:11-15; II Corinthians 5:10 (basis facts)

> It will involve ALL believers — Romans 14:10-13 — v. 10 — *"we shall all stand before the judgment seat of Christ"*

It will involve our personal accountability to God – Romans 14:12 – *"So then every one of us shall give account of himself to God"*

This event should keep us from judging other believers! Romans 14:13 – *"Let us not therefore judge one another any more"*

It will involve the matter of reward!
I Corinthians 3:11-15

It will involve all that we have done in this life – whether good or bad!
II Corinthians 5:10

JUDGMENT OF THE NATIONS – Matthew 25:31-46

Comes at the end of the Tribulation – 25:31 – *"When the Son of man shall come in His glory"*

It will involve ALL nations – 25:32 – *"and before Him shall be gathered all nations"*

It is based on the treatment of His people – 25:40 – *"Inasmuch as ye have done it unto one of the least of these My brethren, ye have done it unto Me"*

The consequences are everlasting – 25:46 – *"these shall go away into everlasting punishment: but the righteous into life eternal"*

JUDGMENT OF ISRAEL – Ezekiel 20:34-38

The standards of His covenant will be applied – v. 37 – *"I will bring you into the bond of the covenant"*

The rebels will be purged out – v. 38 – *"And I will purge out from among you the rebels"*

The judgment keeps the rebels from ever enjoying the promised land – v. 38 cf. Zechariah 13:8-9

JUDGMENT OF THE ANTICHRIST AND FALSE PROPHET – Revelation 19:19-20

JUDGMENT OF SATAN –
Revelation 20:10

JUDGMENT OF THE GREAT
WHITE THRONE – non-believers
Revelation 20:11-15

> The basis of the judgment involves two issues:
>
> The "books" involving their "works"
>
> The "book of life" which will involve the lake of fire!
>
> (3) The <u>INTENT</u> behind this gathering of all nations – v. 12

"Let the heathen (nations) be wakened, and come up to the valley of Jehoshaphat: for there sill I sit to judge all the heathen (nations) round about."

The <u>RIPENESS</u> of judgment based on the greatness of their wickedness! v. 13

"Put ye in the sickle, for the harvest is ripe: come, get you down; for the press is full, the vats overflow; for their wickedness is great."

The *"sickle"* can refer to a grape harvester's knife. The word *"ripe"* can mean "boil" and refer to the ripeness of the grapes.

In Isaiah 63:1-6 we have a graphic picture of the Messiah coming to judge the nations of the world for their treatment of God's people. Take a moment right now and read this amazing prophecy:

"Who is this that cometh from Edom, with dyed garments from Bozrah? This that is glorious in His apparel, travelling in the greatness of His strength? I that speak in righteousness, mighty to save. Wherefore art Thou red in Thine apparel, and Thy garments like him that treadeth in the winevat? I have trodden the winepress alone; and of the people there was none with Me: for I will tread them in Mine anger, and trample them in My fury; and their blood shall be sprinkled upon My garments, and I will stain all My

raiment. For the day of vengeance is in Mine heart, and the year of My redeemed is come. And I looked, and there was none to help; and I wondered that there was none to uphold: therefore Mine own arm brought salvation unto Me; and My fury, it upheld Me. And I will tread down the people in Mine anger, and make them drunk in My fury, and I will bring down their strength to the earth."

WHAT AN AMAZING AND INSIGHTFUL PROPHECY!

The Messiah's garments are *"red"* like the juice of the grapes that are being trampled in an ancient winepress. The color is that of the blood that will be poured out, the blood of all the nations of the world – this day is coming – make no mistake about it!

In Revelation 14:18-20 we have similar words:

"And another angel came out from the altar, which had power over fire; and cried with a loud cry to him that had the sharp sickle, saying, Thrust in thy sharp sickle, and gather the clusters of

the vine of the earth; for her grapes are fully ripe. And the angel thrust in his sickle into the earth, and gathered the vine of the earth, and cast it into the great winepress of the wrath of God. And the winepress was trodden without the city, and blood came out of the winepress, even unto the horse bridles, by the space of a thousand and six hundred furlongs (approximately 180 to 200 miles)."

This bloodbath occurs at the end of the coming Day of the LORD (a period of seven years) when the Messiah returns and delivers His people who are being attacked by the nations of the world.

Zechariah 14:1-3 states clearly what is soon to occur on planet earth:

"Behold, the day of the LORD cometh, and thy spoil shall be divided in the midst of thee. For I will gather all nations against Jerusalem to battle; and the city shall be taken, and the houses rifled, and the women ravished (raped); *and half of the city shall go forth into captivity, and the residue of the people shall not be cut off from the city. Then shall the LORD go forth, and*

fight against those nations, as when He fought in the day of battle."

The <u>REALIZATION</u> that the Day of the Lord has come!
Joel 3:14-15

"Multitudes, multitudes in the valley of decision: for the day of the LORD is near in the valley of decision. The sun and the moon shall be darkened, and the stars shall withdraw their shining."

The <u>ROARING</u> of the LORD will announce His intervention for the sake of His own people!
Joel 3:16

"The LORD also shall roar out of Zion, and utter His voice from Jerusalem; and the heavens and the earth shall shake: but the LORD will be the hope of His people, and the strength of the children of Israel."

Amos 1:2 – *"And he said, The LORD shall roar from Zion, and utter His voice from Jerusalem; and the inhabitations of the shepherds shall mourn, and the top of Carmel shall wither."*

(1) He is the <u>STRENGTH</u> that will defeat all of Israel's enemies! *"the heavens and the earth shall shake"*

(2) He is the <u>SECURITY</u> of His people! *"the LORD will be the hope of His people"*

(3) He is the <u>STRONGHOLD</u> where they can hide and find shelter! *"the strength of the children of Israel"*

The <u>RECOGNITION</u> of the LORD will be obvious to His people! Joel 3:17-21

"So shall ye know that I am the LORD your God dwelling in Zion, My holy mountain: then shall Jerusalem be holy, and there shall no strangers pass through her anymore. And it shall come to pass in that day, that the mountains shall drop down new wine, and the hills shall flow with milk, and all the rivers of Judah shall flow with waters, and a fountain shall come forth

of the house of the LORD, and shall water the valley of Shittim (acacia trees – Sinai desert). *Egypt shall be a desolation, and Edom shall be a desolate wilderness, for the violence against the children of Judah, because they have shed innocent blood in their land. But Judah shall dwell forever, and Jerusalem from generation to generation. For I will cleanse their blood that I have not cleansed: for the LORD dwelleth in Zion."*

1. The <u>PRESENCE</u> of the LORD in Zion brings the hope and comfort of the LORD to His people!

v. 17 – *"I am the LORD your God dwelling in Zion"*
v. 21 – *"for the LORD dwelleth in Zion"*

2. The <u>PRODUCTIVITY</u> of the Land is a remarkable change that God's people will experience! – v. 18 – *"from the house of the LORD"*

3. The <u>PUNISHMENT</u> of their enemies will be executed by the LORD! v. 19
"for the violence against the children of Judah, because they

have shed innocent blood in their land.

4. The <u>PERMANENCE</u> of the people and their city is guaranteed! – v. 20 – *"But Judah shall dwell forever, and Jerusalem from generation to generation."*

5. The <u>PARDON</u> of all their sin will take place – v. 21 – *"For I will cleanse their blood that I have not cleansed: for the LORD dwelleth in Zion."*

Zechariah 13:1 adds: *"In that day there shall be a fountain opened to the house of David and to the inhabitants of Jerusalem for sin and for uncleanness."*

Chapter 8
THE DAY OF GOD'S WRATH

Thousands of people, both Jewish and Christian, believe that God loves every person equally whether they believe in Him or not. This is simply NOT true!
This kind of reasoning argues that God does not hate anyone. That also is NOT true!

Psalm 5:4-5
"For Thou art NOT a God that hath pleasure in wickedness: neither shall evil dwell with Thee. The foolish shall not stand in Thy sight: Thou hatest all workers of iniquity."

Psalm 7:11
"God judgeth the righteous, and God is angry with the wicked every day."

Psalm 9:17
"The wicked shall be turned into hell, and all the nations that forget God."

Psalm 11:5
"The LORD trieth the righteous: but the wicked and him that loveth violence His soul hateth."

Psalm 14:1-3
"The fool hath said in his heart, There is no God. They are corrupt, they have done abominable works, there is none that doeth good. The LORD looked down from heaven upon the children of men, to see if there were any that did understand, and seek God. They are all gone aside, they are all together become filthy: there is none that doeth good, no, not one."

Psalm 34:16
"The face of the LORD is against them that do evil, to cut off the remembrance of them from the earth."

Psalm 37:1-2
"Fret not thyself because of evildoers, neither be thou envious against the workers of iniquity. For they shall soon be cut down like the grass, and wither as the green herb."

In addition to the above verses that prove God, in fact, does not love everyone the same, the Bible also clearly teaches that God hates the workers of iniquity. Malachi 1:2-3 reveals that God *"loved Jacob"* but *"hated Esau."*

THE BIBLE TEACHES THAT THE COMING DAY OF THE LORD IS A DAY OF WRATH, NOT BLESSING!

Revelation 6:12-17 describes the opening of the sixth seal judgment. Revelation pictures three sets of judgments:
> SEVEN SEALS
> SEVEN TRUMPETS
> SEVEN BOWLS

When the sixth seal is opening, Revelation 6:12-17 tells us:

"Lo, there was a great earthquake; and the sun became black as sackcloth of hair, and the moon became as blood; and the stars of heaven fell unto the earth, even as a fig tree casteth her untimely figs, when she is shaken of a mighty wind. And the heaven departed as a scroll when it is rolled together; and every mountain and island were moved out of their places. And the kings of the earth, and the great men, and the rich men, and the chief captains, and the mighty men, and every bondman, and every free man, hid themselves in the dens and in the rocks of the mountains; and said to the mountains and rocks, Fall on us, and

hide us from the face of Him that sitteth on the throne, and from the WRATH of the Lamb: For the great day of His WRATH is come; and who shall be able to stand?"

In Revelation 15:7 we are told that the seven angels mentioned in these prophecies were given *"seven golden vials (bowls) full of the wrath of God, Who liveth forever and ever."*

Revelation 16:1 says: *"And I heard a great voice out of the temple saying to the seven angels, Go your ways, and pour out the vials of the WRATH of God upon the earth."*

There are 84 usages of the word *"great"* in the Book of Revelation, and 11 of them in chapter 16.

WHAT ARE THE SEVEN BOWLS OF WRATH?

1. A noisome and grievous sore!

Revelation 16:2 – *"And the first went, and poured out his vial upon the earth; and there fell a noisome and grievous sore upon the men which had the mark of the beast, and upon them which worshipped his image."*

This attack upon the health of the unbelievers of planet earth reminds us of what happened when Israel was in bondage to Egypt. In Exodus 9:8-11 we read:

"And the LORD said unto Moses and unto Aaron, Take to you handfuls of ashes of the furnace, and let Moses sprinkle it toward the heaven in the sight of Pharaoh. And it shall become small dust in all the land of Egypt, and shall be a boil breaking forth with blains upon man, and upon beast, throughout all the land of Egypt. And they took ashes of the furnace, and stood before Pharaoh; and Moses sprinkled it up toward heaven; and it became a boil breaking forth with blains (blisters) *upon man, and upon beast. And the magicians could not stand before Moses because of the boils; for the boil was upon the magicians, and upon all the Egyptians."*

This *"sore"* was very painful. It is possible that this was a result of the mark of the beast, perhaps a malignant sore like cancer, or was it radiation from nuclear or atomic fallout! We just don't know, but the health of the planet is being attacked by the wrath of Almighty God!

2. Death of sea creatures!

Revelation 16:3 – *"And the second angel poured out his vial upon the sea; and it became as the blood of a dead man; and every living soul died in the sea."*

Once again, the similarity to the plagues of Egypt is striking indeed. We read in Exodus 7:19-21:

"And the LORD spake unto Moses, Say unto Aaron, Take thy rod, and stretch out thine hand upon the waters of Egypt, upon their streams, upon their rivers, and upon their ponds, and upon all their pools of water, that they may become blood; and that there may be blood throughout all the land of Egypt, both in vessels of wood, and in vessels of stone. And Moses and Aaron did so, as the LORD commanded; and he lifted up the rod, and smote the waters that were in the river, in the sight of

Pharaoh, and in the sight of his servants; and all the waters that were in the river were turned to blood. And the fish that was in the river died; and the river stank, and the Egyptians could not drink of the water of the river; and there was blood throughout all the land of Egypt."

Also, back at the trumpet judgments something similar happened – Revelation 8:8-9:

"And the second angel sounded, and as it were a great mountain burning with fire was cast into the sea; and the third part of the sea became blood; and the third part of the creatures which were in the sea, and had life, died; and the third part of the ships were destroyed."

This second trumpet judgment was not as extensive as the second bowl of wrath judgment, and the details are different. However, what happened in Egypt, and what will happen at the second trumpet judgment are the result of the wrath of God!

Obviously, the food supply of planet earth has been greatly affected by this judgment from the LORD God of Israel!

3. Rivers and fountains become blood!

This third judgment strikes at drinking water. Revelation 16:4-7 gives us an interesting look at how the *"angel of the waters"* responded as well as *"another out of the altar."*

"And the third angel poured out his vial upon the rivers and fountains of waters; and they became blood. And I heard the angel of the waters say, Thou art righteous, O Lord, which art, and wast, and shalt be, because thou hast judged thus. For they have shed the blood of saints and prophets, and Thou hast given them blood to drink; for they are worthy. And I heard another out of the altar say, Even so, Lord God Almighty, true and righteous are Thy judgments."

This particular judgment of the wrath of God brings the praise and exaltation of the angel! They proclaim that the LORD

God is righteous because He has brought this judgment upon planet earth!

4. Men are scorched with fire!

Revelation 16:8-9 – *"And the fourth angel poured out his vial upon the sun; and power was given unto him to scorch men with fire. And men were scorched with great heat, and blasphemed the Name of God, which hath power over these plagues: and they repented not to give Him glory."*

The phrase *"the men"* back in verse 2 is referring to those who took the *"mark of the beast"* and *"worshipped his image."*

It is obvious that the problem with the world is not the environment but the human heart that refuses to repent!

5. Full of darkness!

Revelation 16:10-11 – *"And the fifth angel poured out his vial upon the seat of the beast; and his kingdom was full of darkness; and they gnawed their tongues for pain, and blasphemed the God of heaven because of their pains and their sores, and repented not of their deeds.*

Notice five things about this attack upon energy sources:

> (1) It is a <u>REMINDER</u> of what happened in Egypt!

Exodus 10:21-23 – *"And the LORD said unto Moses, Stretch out thine hand toward heaven, that there may be darkness over the land of Egypt, even darkness which may be felt. And Moses stretched forth his hand toward heaven; and there was a thick darkness in all the land of Egypt three days: They saw not one another, neither rose any from his place for three days: but all the children of Israel had light in their dwellings."*

> (2) It is a <u>RESULT</u> that previews hell itself!

Matthew 25:30 – *"And cast ye the unprofitable servant into outer darkness: there shall be weeping and gnashing of teeth."*

(3)　　It is a <u>REACTION</u> of those who worship the beast and his image!

"blasphemed the God of heaven"

(4)　　It is a <u>RESPONSE</u> to their pains and sores!

"because of their pains and their sores"

(5)　　It is <u>REFUSAL</u> to repent!

"and repented not of their deeds"

6. Euphrates river dried up
7. and the coming of ARMAGEDDON!

Revelation 16:12-16 – *"And the sixth angel poured out his vial upon the great river Euphrates; and the water thereof was dried up, that the way of the kings of the east might be prepared. And I saw three unclean spirits like frogs come out of the mouth of the dragon, and out of the mouth of the beast, and out of the mouth of the false prophet. For they are the spirits of devils, working miracles, which go forth unto the kings of the earth and of the whole world, to gather them to the battle of that great day of God Almighty. Behold, I come as a thief. Blessed is he that watcheth, and keepeth his garments, lest he walk naked, And they see his shame. And He gathered them together into a place called in the Hebrew tongue Armageddon."*

Notice four things about this sixth bowl of wrath:

(1)   The **PREPARATION** of this battle – v. 12

"the great river Euphrates, and the water thereof was dried up that the way of the kings of the east might be prepared."

Is it possible that there is a connection with the sixth trumpet judgment of Revelation 9:13-16?:

"And the sixth angel sounded, and I heard a voice from the hour horns of the golden altar with is before God, Saying to the sixth angel which had the trumpet, Loose the four angels which are bound in the great river Euphrates.

And the four angels were loosed, which were prepared for an hour, and a day, and a month, and a year, for to slay the third part of men. And the number of the army of the horsemen were two hundred thousand thousand: and I heard the number of them."

It is possible that these demonic forces are connected to the *"kings of the east"* who will attack Israel in the final days of the tribulation period or the coming DAY of the LORD. Imagine this – 200 million armed forces coming from the *"east"* - or the *"rising of the sun."* It would include the countries of China, South Asia, and surrounding nations.

        (2)   The **PRESENCE** of demonic forces – vv. 13-14a

The reference to *"unclean spirits"* that come out of the mouths of the unholy trinity of the dragon, the beast, and the false prophet – suggest that these *"kings of the east"* are supernatural forces – this creates a major titanic battle between the Lord and Satan and his demons (fallen angels) who inhabit the bodies of these attacking armies of China and Southeast Asia.

These *"unclean spirits"* come with the power to work *"miracles"* and to gather the kings of the earth and of the whole world to the battle of the great day of God Almighty!

> (3) The <u>PROMISE</u> of the Second Coming of the Messiah!

His coming will be a total surprise – *"as a thief."* The seriousness of such an event is emphasized by the words *"Blessed is he that watcheth, and keepeth his garments, lest he walk naked, and they see his shame."*

> (4) The <u>PLACE</u> where the nations will be gathered together!

The word "ARMAGEDDON" in the Hebrew language simply means "hill of Megiddo." The word becomes a symbol of war (many battles in history fought at Megiddo, a pass that was necessary to enter in order to proceed further).

Revelation 14 speaks of the entire Land of Israel as the *"winepress of the wrath of God."* The blood will flow up to the bridles of horses and the length of this winepress is described as *"a thousand and six hundred furlongs."* One *"furlong"* is about 600 feet – 1600 furlongs would be about 180 to 200 miles. That happens to be the length of the Land of Israel from Dan (north – foot of Mount Hermon) to Beersheba (south – before entering the Sinai desert).

8. A great earthquake and giant hailstones!

Revelation 16:17-21 – *"And the seventh angel poured out his vial into the air; and there came a great voice out of the temple of heaven, from the throne, saying, It is done! And there were voices, and thunders, and lightnings; and there was a great earthquake, such as was not since men were upon the earth, so mighty an earthquake, and so great. And the great city was divided into three parts, and the cities of the nations fell: and great Babylon came in remembrance before God, to give unto her the cup of the wine of the fierceness of His wrath. And every island fled away, and the mountains were not found. And there fell upon men a great hail out of heaven, every stone about the weight of a talent (about 100 pounds each): and men blasphemed God because of the plague of the hail; for the plague thereof was exceeding great."*

  (1) It will be the <u>COMPLETION</u> of God's plan – v. 17

The *"great voice out of the temple in heaven"* – ÍT IS DONE!" These final seven bowls of wrath will bring to an end the plan of God to unleash His fury and wrath upon planet earth.

  (2) It will be the greatest <u>CATASTROPHE</u> of all time!

This great catastrophe will bring the following disasters:

BABYLON WILL BE DESTROYED!
ALL CITIES FALLEN!
EVERY ISLAND AND ALL MOUNTAINS DISAPPEAR!
GIANT HAILSTONES FALL !

The wrath of Almighty God during this time of tribulation called "THE DAY OF THE LORD" will bring the death of over half of the world's population, and will cause serious health problems, and attacks upon food and drinking water, darkness that can be felt, worldwide damage to the cities of the world, a final battle that will bring all nations of the world against Israel, and a bloodbath that will be greater in damage and death than the world has ever seen!

Chapter 9
THE COMING OF ELIJAH

One of the great prophecies about the coming DAY of the LORD is the prediction that Elijah the prophet will come before that awful DAY of the LORD arrives. The prophet MALACHI is the one who brings this prediction to our attention.

THE DAY OF THE LORD IS COMING!
Malachi 4:1-6

The <u>CONSEQUENCES</u> for the wicked – Malachi 4:1

"For, behold, the day cometh, that shall burn as an oven; and all the proud, yea, and all that do wickedly, shall be stubble: and the day that cometh shall burn them up, saith the LORD of hosts, that it shall leave them neither root nor branch."

1. The DAY it will happen!

"the day cometh" – mentioned twice (cf. Joel 1:15; 2:1)

Zephaniah 1:7 – *"Hold thy peace at the presence of the Lord GOD; for the day of the LORD is at hand: for the LORD hath prepared a sacrifice, He hath bid His guests."*

Zephaniah 1:14-15 – *"The great day of the LORD is near, it is near, and hasteth greatly, even the voice of the day of the LORD: the mighty man shall cry there bitterly. That day is a day of wrath, a day of trouble and distress, a day of wasteness and desolation, a day of darkness and gloominess, a day of clouds and thick darkness."*

I Thessalonians 5:1-3 – *"But of the times and the seasons, brethren, ye have no need that I write unto you. For yourselves know perfectly that the day of the Lord so cometh as a thief in the night. For when they shall say, Peace and safety; then sudden destruction cometh upon them, as travail upon a woman with child; and they shall not escape."*

2. The DESTRUCTION that will take place! - "burn as an oven" and "burn them up"

Isaiah 30:27 – *"Behold, the Name of the LORD cometh from far, burning with His anger, and the burden thereof is heavy: His lips are full of indignation, and His tongue as a devouring fire."*

3. The DEEDS that will be punished!
"all the proud, yea, and all that do wickedly"

NOTE: Hebrew word for "proud" – *zadim* and for "do wickedly"

Malachi 3:15 – *"And now we call the proud happy; yea, they that work wickedness are set up; yea, they that tempt God are even delivered."*

4.Their DESCENDANTS will no longer exist!
"it shall leave them neither root nor branch"

The CHARACTER of the Messiah

Malachi 4:2

"But unto you that fear My Name shall the Sun of righteousness arise with healing in His wings: and ye shall go forth, and grow up as calves of the stall."

1. The PEOPLE that shall be healed!
"fear My Name"

Malachi 3:16 – *"Then they that feared the LORD spake often one to another: and the LORD hearkened, and heard it, and a book of remembrance was written before Him for them that feared the LORD, and that thought upon His Name."*

2. The PERSON Who heals them!
"Sun of righteousness"

Isaiah 30:26 – *"Moreover the light of the moon shall be as the light of the sun, and the light of the sun shall be sevenfold, as the light of seven days, in the day that the LORD bindeth up the breach of His people, and healeth the stroke of their wound."*

Isaiah 60:1-3 – *"Arise, shine; for thy light is come, and the glory of the LORD is risen upon thee. For, behold, the darkness shall cover the earth, and gross darkness the people: but the LORD shall arise upon thee, and His glory shall be seen upon thee. And the Gentiles shall come to Thy light, and kings to the brightness of Thy rising."*

NOTE: The reference to "wings" could be referring to the rays of the sun.

3. The POWER that will be displayed! *"calves of the stall"*

The figure of calves enjoying open pastures after being in a pen (stall) reveals the future satisfaction and joy of the righteous.

The CONQUEST of the righteous - Malachi 4:3

"And ye shall tread down the wicked; for they shall be ashes under the soles of your feet in the day that I shall do this, saith the LORD of hosts."

1. The ILLUSTRATION that is used

The words *"tread down"* are from a Hebrew root also used of "sweet wine" from the grapes – referring no doubt to the calves treading down the grapes.

2. The INTENT behind this illustration

It pictures total victory and devastation of the wicked – *"ashes under the soles of your feet"*

Isaiah 66:24 – *"And they shall go forth, and look upon the carcases of the men that have transgressed against Me: for their worm shall not die, neither shall their fire be quenched; and they shall be an abhorring unto all flesh."*

Matthew 3:12 – *"Whose fan is in His hand, and He will throughly purge His floor, and gather His wheat into the garner; but He will burn up the chaff with unquenchable fire."*

Mark 9:48 – *"Where their worm dieth not, and the fire is not quenched."*

The IMPACT is supernatural!
"in the day that I shall do this"

1. **It was a CHARGE to remember!**

Malachi 4:4 – *"Remember ye the law of Moses My servant"*

2. **It was the COMMAND of the LORD Himself!**

Malachi 4:4a – *"which I commanded unto him in Horeb for all Israel..."*

3. **It was the CONDUCT for all Israel**

"the statutes" – Heb: huqqim
"judgments" – Heb: mishpatim

The COMING of Elijah

Malachi 4:5-6 – *"Behold, I will send you Elijah the prophet before the coming of the great and dreadful day of the LORD: And he shall turn the heart of the fathers to the children, and the heart of the children to their fathers, lest I come and smite the earth with a curse."*

1. The TRUTH about Elijah

NOTE: In Malachi 4:5-6 it speaks of "Elijah" and places it in an eschatological context of the Second Coming of our Lord; but the NT argues that if Israel repents at the preaching of John the Baptist, then he is the "Elijah."

Elijah is the most frequently mentioned (30 times) OT person after Moses (80 times), Abraham (73), and David (59). There are ten clear references to Elijah in the Synoptic Gospels (Matthew, Mark, & Luke) and one indirect connection in John 1:21, 25.

There is also the connection made in Revelation 11:3-13 with the "two witnesses" of Zechariah 4:14.

Matthew 3:1-3 and Luke 3:2-6 – connects John the Baptist with the prophecy of Isaiah 40:3-5

Luke 4:25-26 – refers to Elijah's visit to the widow in Sidon

Mark 6:14-16 – incident with Herod about the death of John the Baptist

Matthew 16:13-14; Mark 8:27-30 – at Caesarea Philippi

Matthew 17:3-4; Mark 9:4-5; Luke 9:30, 33 - Mt. of Transfiguration

Matthew 17:10-13; Mark 9:11-13 – disciples asked about the scribes' belief that Elijah must come first.

Luke 1:15-17 – Zacharias about the birth of John the Baptist

Luke 9:54-56 – *"command fire to come down from heaven, and consume them, even as Elijah did?"*

Matthew 11:7-15 – remarks of Yeshua to His disciples about the connection of John the Baptist with Elijah.

Matthew 27:46-47 – words of Yeshua on the cross from Psalm 22:1.

WHAT WE LEARN FROM THESE PASSAGES

Some people thought that Yeshua might be Elijah – He made it clear that He was not Elijah!

Elijah is identified as the *"voice...crying in the wilderness"* in Isaiah's prophecy.

John the Baptist is referred to as the one who will come *"in the spirit and power of Elijah"* and *"turn"* many *"to the Lord their God"* – connecting him to the prophecy of Malachi 4:6.

Yeshua said (Matthew 11:14) *"if ye will receive it, this is Elijah, which was for to come"*

Yeshua said (Matthew 17:12-13) that *"Elijah is come already, and they knew him not"* – the disciples understood that He was referring to John the Baptist.

Yeshua said (Mark 9:12) that *"Elijah verily cometh first and restoreth all things"* and *"Elijah is indeed come."*

If Elijah is one of the two witnesses, then he must still come before the Messiah returns!

2. The TIMING of his coming
"<u>before</u> the coming of the great and dreadful day of the LORD"

3. The TURNING of hearts

Luke 1:15-17 – *"For he shall be great in the sight of the Lord, and shall drink neither wine nor strong drink; and he shall be filled with the Holy Ghost, even from his mother's womb. And many of the children of Israel shall he turn to the Lord their God. And he shall go before Him in the spirit and power of Elijah, to turn the hearts of the fathers to the children, and the disobedient to the wisdom of the just; to make ready a people prepared for the Lord."*

4. The TRAGEDY that may result
"smite the earth with a curse"

Hebrew: *herem* – "ban" – refers to the judgment of God

Chapter 10
WHAT IS THE DAY
OF THE LORD?

THE DAY OF THE LORD IS NEAR!
This is clearly the warning we are given by the Hebrew prophet Zephaniah.

Zephaniah 1:14-18
"The great day of the LORD is near, it is near, and hasteth greatly, even the voice of the day of the LORD: the mighty man shall cry there bitterly. That day is a day of wrath, a day of trouble and distress, a day of wasteness and desolation, a day of darkness and gloominess, a day of clouds and thick darkness, A day of the trumpet and alarm against the fenced cities, and against the high towers. And I will bring distress upon men, that they shall walk like blind men, because they have sinned against the LORD: and their blood shall be poured out as dust, and their flesh as the dung. Neither their silver nor their gold shall be able to deliver them in the day of the LORD's wrath; but the whole land shall be devoured by the fire of His jealousy: for

He shall make even a speedy riddance of all them that dwell in the land."

The phrase "in that day" is used 115 times (43 in Isaiah alone!) – seven times in the New Testament. It is an eschatological term that refers the majority of times to the coming "Day of the LORD" or the "tribulation" and the "Second Coming" of the Messiah, and His kingdom on earth.

Revelation 6:17 – *"For the great day of His wrath is come; and who shall be able to stand?"*

Revelation 16:14 speaks of *"the battle of that great day of God Almighty."*

THE MEANING OF THE DAY OF THE LORD

1. It is the LORD's REVENGE!

Isaiah 63:1-6 – *"Who is this that cometh from Edom, with dyed garments from Bozrah? This that is glorious in His apparel, travelling in the greatness of His strength? I that speak in righteousness, mighty to save. Wherefore art Thou red in Thine apparel, and Thy garments like him that treadeth in the winevat? I have trodden the winepress alone; and of the people there was none with Me: for I will tread them in Mine anger, and trample them in My fury; and their blood shall be sprinkled upon My garments, and I will stain all My raiment. For the day of vengeance is in Mine heart, and the year of My redeemed is come. And I looked, and there was none to help; and I wondered that there was none to uphold: therefore Mine own arm brought salvation unto Me; and My fury, it upheld Me. And I will tread down the people in Mine anger, and make them drunk in My fury, and I will bring down their strength to the earth."*

Ezekiel 38:19 – *"For in My jealousy and in the fire of My wrath have I spoken, surely in that day there shall be a great shaking in the land of Israel."*

Nahum 1:2-7 – *"God is jealous, and the LORD revengeth; the LORD revengeth, and is furious; the LORD will take vengeance on His adversaries, and He reserveth wrath for His enemies. The LORD is slow to anger, and great in* power, and will not at all acquit the wicked: the LORD hath His way in the whirlwind and in the storm, and the clouds are the dust of His feet. He rebuketh the sea, and maketh it dry, and drieth up all the rivers: Bashan languisheth, and Carmel, and the flower of Lebanon languisheth. The mountains quake at Him, and the hills melt, and the earth is burned at His presence, yea, the world, and all that dwell therein. Who can stand before His indignation? And who can abide in the fierceness of His anger? His fury is poured out like fire, and the rocks are thrown down by Him. The LORD is good, a stronghold in the day of trouble; and He knoweth them that trust in Him."

2. It is the LORD's REVELATION of Himself!

Ezekiel 38:23 – "Thus will I magnify Myself, and sanctify Myself; and I will be known in the eyes of many nations, and they shall know that I am the LORD."

Ezekiel 39:21-22 – "And I will set My glory among the heathen, and all the heathen shall see My judgment that I have executed, and My hand that I have laid upon them. So the house of Israel shall know that I am the LORD their God from that day and forward."

Joel 3:16-17 – "The LORD also shall roar out of Zion, and utter His voice from Jerusalem; and the heavens and the earth shall shake: but the LORD will be the hope of His people, and the strength of the children of Israel. So shall ye know that I am the LORD your God dwelling in Zion, My holy mountain: then shall Jerusalem be holy, and there shall no strangers pass through her anymore."

3. It is the LORD's REFINING of His people!

Daniel 12:10 – "Many shall be purified, and made white, and tried; but the wicked shall do wickedly: and none of the wicked shall understand; but the wise shall understand."

Malachi 3:2-3 – "But who may abide the day of His coming? And who shall stand when He appeareth? For He is like a refiner's fire, and like fullers' *soap: And He shall sit as a refiner and purified of silver: and He shall purify the sons of Levi, and purge them as gold and silver, that they may offer unto the LORD an offering in righteousness."*

4. It is the LORD's REACTION against all who have sinned against Him!

Zephaniah 1:14-18 – *"The great day of the LORD is near, it is near, and hasteth greatly; even the voice of the day of the LORD: the mighty man shall cry there bitterly. That day is a day of wrath, a day of trouble and distress, a day of wasteness and desolation, a day of darkness and gloominess, a day of clouds and thick darkness, a day of the trumpet and alarm against the fenced cities, and against the high towers. And I will bring distress upon men, that they shall walk like blind men, because they have sinned against the LORD: and their blood shall be poured out as dust, and their flesh as the dung. Neither their silver nor their gold shall be able to deliver them in the day of the LORD's wrath; but the whole land shall be devoured by the fire of His jealousy: for*

He shall make even a speedy riddance of all them that dwell in the land."

5. It is the LORD's RENNOVATION of the entire planet!

II Peter 3:10-13 – *"But the day of the LORD will come as a thief in the night; in the which the heavens shall pass away with a great noise, and the elements shall melt with fervent heat, the earth also and the works that are therein shall be burned up. Seeing then that all these things shall be dissolved, what manner of persons ought ye to be in all holy conversation and godliness, Looking for and hasting unto the coming of the day of God, wherein the heavens being on fire shall be dissolved, and the elements shall melt with fervent heat? Nevertheless we, according to His promise, look for new heavens and a new earth, wherein dwelleth righteousness."*

THE MOTIVES BEHIND THE DAY OF THE LORD

1. The PROBLEM of Jerusalem will be decided!

Zechariah 12:1-3 – *"The burden of the word of the LORD for Israel, saith the LORD, which stretcheth forth the heavens, and layeth the foundation of the earth, and formeth the spirit of man within him. Behold, I will make Jerusalem a cup of trembling unto all the people round about, when they shall be in the siege both against Judah and against Jerusalem. And in that day will I make Jerusalem a burdensome stone for all people: all that burden themselves with it shall be cut in pieces, though all the people of the earth be gathered together against it."*

2. The POWER of God will be displayed!

Isaiah 13:9-13 – *"Behold, the day of the LORD cometh, cruel both with wrath and fierce anger, to lay the land desolate: and He shall destroy the sinners thereof out of it. For the stars of heaven and the constellations thereof shall not give their light: the sun shall be darkened in his going forth, and the moon shall not cause her light to shine.*

And I will punish the world for their evil, and the wicked for their iniquity; and I will cause the arrogancy of the proud to cease, and will lay low the haughtiness of the terrible. I will make a man more precious that fine gold; even a man than the golden wedge of Ophir. Therefore I will shake the heavens, and the earth shall remove out of her place, in the wrath of the LORD of hosts, and in the day of His fierce anger."

Ezekiel 38:23 – *"Thus will I magnify Myself, and sanctify Myself; and I will be known in the eyes of many nations, and they shall know that I am the LORD."*

3. The PEOPLE of Israel shall be delivered!

Ezekiel 37:25-28 – *"And they shall dwell in the land that I have given unto Jacob My servant, wherein your fathers have dwelt; and they shall dwell therein, even they, and their children, and their children's children forever: and My servant David shall be their prince forever. Moreover I will make a covenant of peace with them; it shall be* an everlasting covenant with them: yea, I will be their God, and they shall be My people. And the heathen shall know that I the LORD do sanctify Israel, when My sanctuary shall be in the midst of them for evermore."

Joel 2:32 – "And it shall come to pass, that whosoever shall call on the Name of the LORD shall be delivered: for in mount Zion and in Jerusalem shall be deliverance as the LORD hath said, and in the remnant whom the LORD shall call."

Zechariah 12:10 – "And I will pour upon the house of David, and upon the inhabitants of Jerusalem, the spirit of grace and of supplications: and they shall look upon Me Whom they have pierced, and they shall mourn for Him, as one mourneth for his only son, and shall be in bitterness for Him, as one that is in bitterness for his firstborn."

Zechariah 13:1 – "In that day there shall be a fountain opened to the house of David and to the inhabitants of Jerusalem for sin and for uncleanness."

Romans 11:25-27 – *"For I would not, brethren, that ye should be ignorant of this mystery, lest ye should be wise in your own conceits, that blindness in part is happened to Israel, until the fullness of the Gentiles be come in. And so all Israel shall be saved: as it is written, There shall come out of Sion the Deliverer, and shall turn away ungodliness from Jacob: For this is My covenant unto them, when I shall take away their sins."*

4. The PERSON of the Messiah will be declared!

Isaiah 45:22-25 – *"Look unto Me, and be ye saved, all the ends of the earth: for I am God, and there is none else. I have sworn by Myself, the word is gone out of My mouth in righteousness, and shall not return, That unto Me every knee shall bow, every tongue shall swear. Surely, shall one say, in the LORD have I righteousness and strength: even to Him shall men come; and all that are incensed against Him shall be ashamed. In the LORD shall all the seed of Israel be justified, and shall glory."*

Phil,

Zechariah 14:9 – *"And the LORD shall be king over all the earth: in that day shall there be one Lord, and His Name one."*

Revelation 11:15-16 – *"And the seventh angel sounded; and there were great voices in heaven, saying, The kingdoms of this world are become the kingdom of our Lord, and of His Christ; and He shall reign forever and ever."*

Revelation 19:16 – *"And He hath on His vesture and on His thigh a name written, KING OF KINGS, AND LORD OF LORDS."*

5. The PROMISES of God will be done!

Isaiah 46:9-11 – *"Remember the former things of old: for I am God, and there is none else; I am God, and there is none like Me, declaring the end from the beginning, and from ancient times the things that are not yet done, saying, My counsel shall stand, and I will do all My pleasure: Calling a ravenous bird from the east, the man that executeth My counsel from a far country: yea, I have* *spoken it, I will also bring it to pass; I have purposed it, I will also do it."*

The whole story of the coming DAY OF THE LORD reveals the control, purposes, and power of Almighty God!

World events and leaders are in His hands. The hearts of wicked rulers can be turned in whatever way the LORD GOD of ISRAEL decides to do.

One question remains – ARE YOU READY FOR THE COMING OF THE DAY OF THE LORD?

Chapter 11
ARE YOU READY FOR THE COMING OF THE DAY OF THE LORD?

It is critical that we answer the above question in the light of the prophecies of the Bible concerning the coming DAY of the LORD.

REMEMBER WHO IS REALLY IN CHARGE OF WHAT'S HAPPENING!

Amos 4:13 - *"The LORD, the God of hosts, is His name"*

Daniel 4:34-35 – *"And at the end of the days, I, Nebuchadnezzar, lifted up mine eyes unto heaven, and mine understanding returned unto me, and I blessed the Most High, and I praised and honored Him Who liveth forever, Whose dominion is an everlasting dominion, and His kingdom is from generation to generation. And all the inhabitants of the earth are reputed as nothing; and He doeth according to His will in the army of heaven, and among the inhabitants of the earth, and none can stay His hand, or say unto Him, What doest Thou?"*

Psalm 99:1-3 – *"The LORD reigneth; let the people tremble. He sitteth between the cherubim; let the earth be moved. The LORD is great in Zion, and He is high above all the peoples. Let them praise Thy great and terrible Name; for it is holy."*

Psalm 115:3 – *"But our God is in the heavens; He hath done whatsoever He hath pleased."*

Psalm 135:5-6 – *"For I know that the LORD is great, and that our Lord is above all gods. Whatsoever the LORD pleased, that did He is heaven, and in earth."*

REFUSE TO BE DECEIVED!

About the PEACE in the Middle East

Ezekiel 13:8-10 – *"Therefore, thus saith the Lord GOD: Because ye have spoken vanity, and seen lies, therefore, behold, I am against you, saith the Lord GOD.*

And Mine hand shall be upon the prophets that see vanity, and that divine lies; they shall not be in the assembly of My people, neither shall they be written in the writing of the house of Israel, neither shall they enter into the land of Israel; and ye shall know that I am the Lord GOD. Because, even because they have seduced My people, saying, Peace; and there is no peace"

I Thessalonians 5:1-3 – *"But of the times and the seasons, brethren, ye have no need that I write unto you. For yourselves know perfectly that the day of the Lord so cometh as a thief in the night. For when they shall say, Peace and safety, then sudden destruction cometh upon them, as travail upon a woman with child, and they shall not escape."*

About the PERFORMANCE of miracles

Matthew 24:4-5 – *"Take heed that no man deceive you. For many shall come in My Name, saying, I am Christ; and shall deceive many."*

Matthew 24:11 — *"And many false prophets shall rise, and shall deceive many."*

Matthew 24:24 — *"For there shall arise false christs, and false prophets, and shall shew great signs and wonders, insomuch that, if it were possible, they shall deceive the very elect."*

II Thessalonians 2:9-12 — *"Even him whose coming is after the working of Satan with all power and signs and lying wonders, and with all deceivableness of unrighteousness in them that perish, because they received not the love of the truth, that they might be saved. And for this cause God shall send them strong delusion, that they should believe a (the) lie. That they all might be damned who believed not the truth, but had pleasure in unrighteousness."*

Revelation 13:13-14 — *"And he doeth great wonders, so that he maketh fire come down from heaven on the earth in the sight of men, and deceiveth them that dwell on the earth by the means of those miracles which he had power to do in the sight of the beast, saying to them that dwell on the earth, that they should make an image to the beast, that had the wound by a sword, and did live."*

About the PLAN of God for Israel -

Romans 11:1-2a – *"I say then, Hath God cast away His people? God forbid. For I also am an Israelite, of the seed of Abraham, of the tribe of Benjamin. God hath not cast away His people whom He foreknew."*

Romans 11:25-27 – *"For I would not, brethren, that ye should be ignorant of this mystery, lest ye should be wise in your own conceits: that blindness in part is happened to Israel, until the fullness of the Gentiles be come in. and so all Israel shall be saved; as it is written, There shall come out of Zion the Deliverer, and shall turn away ungodliness from Jacob; For this is My covenant unto them, when I shall take away their sins."*

About the PROMISES of God

1. The TRUTH about the Land

Ezekiel 37:11-14 – *"Then He said unto me, Son of man, these bones are the whole house of Israel; behold, they say, Our bones are dried, and our hope is lost; we are cut off for our parts. Therefore, prophesy and say unto them, Thus saith the Lord GOD: Behold, O My people, I will open your graves, and cause you to come up out of your graves, and bring you into the land of Israel. And ye shall know that I am the LORD, when I have opened your graves, O My people, and brought you up out of your graves, and shall put My Spirit in you, and ye shall live, and I shall place you in your own land; then shall ye know that I, the LORD, have spoken it, and performed it, saith the LORD."*

Amos 9:13-15 – *"Behold, the days come, saith the LORD, that the plowman shall overtake the reaper, and the treader of grapes him that soweth seed; and the mountains shall drop sweet wine, and all the hills shall melt. And I will bring again the captivity of My people of Israel, and they shall build the waste cities, and inhabit them; and they shall plant vineyards, and drink their wine; they shall also make gardens, and eat the fruit of them. And I will plant them upon their land, and they shall no more be pulled up out of their land which I have given them, saith the LORD, thy God."*

2. The TEACHING about resurrection

Daniel 12:1-3 – *"And at that time shall Michael stand up, the great prince who standeth for the children of My people, and there shall be a time of trouble, such as never was since there was a nation even to that same time; and at that time Thy people shall be delivered, every one that shall be found written in the book. And many of those who sleep in the dust of the earth shall awake, some to everlasting life, and some to shame and everlasting contempt. And they that be wise shall shine like the brightness of the firmament; and they that turn many to righteousness, as the stars forever and ever."*

I Thessalonians 4:16-17 – *"For the Lord Himself shall descend from heaven with a shout, with the voice of the archangel, and with the trump of God; and the dead in Christ shall rise first; Then we who are alive and remain shall be* caught up together with them in the clouds, to meet the Lord in the air; and so shall we ever be with the Lord."

3. The THINGS to come

Isaiah 44:6-8 – *"Thus saith the LORD, the King of Israel, and His Redeemer, the LORD of hosts: I am the first, and I am the last, and beside Me, there is no God. And who, as I, shall call, and shall declare it, and set it in order for me, since I appointed the ancient people? And the things that are coming, and shall come, let them show unto them. Fear not, neither be afraid; have not I told thee from that time, and have declared it? Ye are even My witnesses. Is there a God beside Me? Yea, there is no God; I know not any."*

Isaiah 46:9-11 – *"Remember the former things of old; for I am God, and there is none else; I am God, and there is none like Me, Declaring the end from the beginning, and from ancient times the things that are not yet done, saying, My counsel shall stand, and I will do all My pleasure; Calling a ravenous bird from the east, the man that executeth My counsel from a far country; yea, I have spoken it, I will also bring it to pass; I have purposed it, I will also do it."*

4. The TIMING of the Second Coming

Matthew 24:36 – *"But of that day and hour knoweth no man, no, not the angels of heaven, but My Father only."*

Matthew 24:42 – *"Watch, therefore; for ye know not what hour your Lord doth come."*

Matthew 24:44 – *"Therefore be ye also ready; for in such an hour as ye think not the Son of man cometh."*

II Peter 3:3-4 – *"Knowing this first, that there shall come in the last days scoffers, walking after their own lusts, and saying, Where is the promise of His coming? For since the fathers fell asleep, all things continue as they were from the beginning of the creation."*

II Peter 3:8-9 – *"But, beloved, be not ignorant of this one thing, that one day is with the Lord as a thousand years, and a thousand years as one day. The Lord is not slack concerning His promise, as some men count slackness, but is longsuffering toward us, not willing that any should perish, but that all should come to repentance."*

REALIZE THAT WE ARE FACING SPIRITUAL WARFARE!

Matthew 26:41 – *"Watch and pray, that ye enter not into temptation; the spirit indeed is willing, but the flesh is weak."*

Ephesians 6:10-13 – *"Finally, my brethren, be strong in the Lord, and in the power of His might. Put on the whole armor of God, that ye may be able to stand against the wiles of the devil. For we wrestle not against flesh and blood, but against principalities, against powers, against the rulers of the darkness of this world, against spiritual wickedness in high places. Wherefore, take unto you the whole armor of God, that ye may be able to withstand in the evil day, and having done all, to stand."*

I Peter 5:8-11 – *"Be sober, be vigilant, because your adversary, the devil, like a roaring lion, walketh about, seeking* whom he may devour; Whom resist stedfast in the faith, knowing that the same afflictions are accomplished in your brethren that are in the world. But the God of all grace, Who hath called us unto His eternal glory by Christ Jesus, after ye have suffered awhile, make you perfect, stablish, strengthen, settle you. To Him be glory and dominion forever and ever. Amen.

RESIST THE TEMPTATIONS OF A SECULAR LIFESTYLE!

Luke 21:34-36 – *"And take heed to yourselves, lest at any time your hearts be overcharged with surfeiting and drunkenness, and cares of this life, and so that day come upon you unawares. For as a snare shall it come on all them that dwell on the face of the whole earth. Watch ye therefore, and pray always, that ye may be accounted worthy to escape all these things that shall come to pass, and to stand before the Son of man."*

I Timothy 6:10 – *"For the love of money is the root of all evil: which while some coveted after, they have erred from the faith, and pierced themselves through with many sorrows."*

I Timothy 6:17 – *"Charge them that are rich in this world, that they be not highminded, not trust in uncertain riches, but in the living God Who giveth us richly all things to enjoy."*

Jude 17-19 – *"But, beloved, remember ye the words which were spoken before of the apostles of our Lord Jesus Christ; How that they told you there should be mockers in the last time, who should walk after their own ungodly lusts. These be they who separate themselves, sensual, having not the Spirit."*

REST IN THE LORD'S CONTROL AND CARE OF THE BELIEVER!

Matthew 24:6 - *"See that ye be not troubled"*

Matthew 28:20 - *"Lo, I am with you always, even unto the end of the world"*

John 14:27 – *"Peace I leave with you, My peace I give unto you: not as the world giveth, give I unto you. Let not your heart be troubled, neither let it be afraid."*

Hebrews 13:5 - *"I will never leave thee, nor forsake thee"*

RELY UPON THE WORD OF GOD ALONE!

II Timothy 3:12-17 – *"Yea, and all that will live godly in Christ Jesus shall suffer persecution. But evil men and seducers shall wax worse and worse, deceiving, and being deceived. But continue thou in the things which thou hast learned and hast been assured of, knowing of whom thou hast learned them; And that from a child thou hast known the holy scriptures, which are able to make thee wise unto salvation through faith which is in Christ Jesus. All scripture is given by inspiration of God, and is profitable for doctrine, for reproof, for correction, for instruction in righteousness: That the man of God may be perfect, throughly furnished unto all good works."*

REPENT OF YOUR SIN AND TURN TO THE LORD!

Hosea 6:1 - *"Come, and let us return unto the LORD...for He will heal us"*

Hosea 14:1 - *"O Israel, return unto the LORD, thy God; for thou hast fallen by thine iniquity"* – He says in verse 4 - *"I will heal their backsliding, I will love them freely"*

Joel 2:12-14a – *"Therefore also now, saith the LORD, turn ye even to Me with all your heart, and with fasting, and with weeping, and with mourning: And rend your heart, and not your garments, and turn unto the LORD your God: for He is gracious and merciful, slow to anger, and of great kindness, and repenteth Him of the evil. Who knoweth if He will return and repent, and leave a blessing behind Him?"*

Zechariah 1:3-4 – *"Therefore say thou unto them, Thus saith the LORD of hosts; Turn ye unto Me, saith the LORD of hosts, and I will turn unto you, saith the LORD of hosts. Be ye not as your fathers, unto whom the former prophets have cried, saying, Thus saith the LORD of hosts, Turn ye now from your evil ways, and from your evil doings: but they did not hear, nor hearken unto Me, saith the LORD."*

Malachi 3:7 – *"Return unto Me, and I will return unto you, saith the LORD of hosts."*

II Chronicles 7:14 – *"If My people, which are called by My Name, shall humble themselves, and pray, and seek My face, and turn from their wicked ways; then will I hear from heaven, and will forgive their sin, and will heal their land."*

A QUICK REVIEW OF HOW TO BE READY FOR THE COMING OF THE DAY OF THE LORD!

REMEMBER WHO IS REALLY IN CHARGE OF WHAT'S HAPPENING!

REFUSE TO BE DECEIVED!

REALIZE THAT WE ARE FACING SPIRITUAL WARFARE!

RESIST THE TEMPTATIONS OF A SECULAR LIFESTYLE!

REST IN THE LORD'S CONTROL AND CARE OF THE BELIEVER!

RELY UPON THE WORD OF GOD ALONE!

REPENT OF YOUR SIN AND TURN TO THE LORD!

Chapter 12
A FINAL WORD TO REMEMBER!

I Thessalonians 5:1-11

"But of the times and the seasons, brethren, ye have no need that I write unto you.   For yourselves know perfectly that THE DAY OF THE LORD so cometh as a thief in the night.   For when they shall say, Peace and safety; then sudden destruction cometh upon them, as travail upon a woman with child; and they shall not escape. But ye, brethren, are not in darkness, that that day should overtake you as a thief. Ye are all children of the day; we are not of the night, nor of darkness. Therefore let us not sleep, as do others; but let us watch and be sober. For they that sleep sleep in the night; and they that be drunken are drunken in the night. But let us, who are of the day, be sober, putting on the breastplate of faith and love; and for an helmet, the hope of salvation. For God hath not appointed us to wrath, but to obtain salvation by our Lord Jesus Christ. Who died for us, that, whether we wake or sleep, we should live together with Him.

Wherefore comfort yourselves together, and edify one another, even as also ye do."

THE <u>CONDITIONS</u> IN THE WORLD WHEN THAT DAY COMES WILL DECEIVE MANY PEOPLE!

I Thessalonians 5:3 – *"For when they shall say, Peace and safety; then sudden destruction cometh upon, as travail upon a woman with child; and they shall not escape."*

A most serious warning from the LORD is found in the Book of Deuteronomy – chapter 29, verses 18-20:

"Lest there should be among you man, or woman, or family, or tribe, whose heart turneth away this day from the LORD our God, to go and serve the gods of these nations; lest there should be among you a root that beareth gall and wormwood; And it come to pass, when he heareth the words of this curse, that he bless himself in his heart, saying, I shall have peace, though I walk in the imagination of mine heart, to add

drunkenness to thirst: The LORD will not spare him, but then the anger of the LORD and His jealousy shall smoke against that man, and all the curses that are written in this book shall lie upon him, and the LORD shall blot out his name from under heaven."

The world will be deceived by the measure of peace and safety that will seem to be present. It is the calm before the storm!

THE COMING OF DESTRUCTION WILL BE A TOTAL SURPRISE!

"then sudden destruction cometh upon them, as travail upon a woman with child"

II Thessalonians 1:7-9
"And to you who are troubled – rest with us, when the Lord Jesus shall be revealed from heaven with His mighty angels, in flaming fire taking vengeance on them that know not God, and that obey not the gospel of our Lord Jesus Christ: Who shall be punished with everlasting destruction from the presence of the Lord, and from the glory of His power."

Proverbs 29:1 says: *"He, that being often reproved hardeneth his neck, shall suddenly be destroyed, and that without remedy."*

1. It comes from the <u>SON OF GOD</u>!

Isaiah 13:6 – *"Howl ye; for the day of the LORD is at hand; it shall come as a destruction from the Almighty."*

Isaiah 63:4-6 – *"For the day of vengeance is in Mine heart, and the year of My redeemed is come. And I looked, and there was none to help; and I wondered that there was none to uphold: therefore Mine own arm brought salvation unto Me; and My fury, it upheld Me. And I will tread down the people in Mine anger, and make them drunk in My fury, and I will bring down their strength to the earth."*

Joel 1:15 – *"Alas for the day! For the day of the LORD is at hand, and as a destruction from the Almighty shall it come."*

Jeremiah 46:10 – *"For this is the day of the LORD God of hosts, a day of* vengeance, the He may avenge Him of His adversaries: and the sword shall devour, and it shall be satiate and made drunk with their blood: for the Lord GOD of hosts hath a sacrifice in the north country by the river Euphrates."

Revelation 19:15 – "And out of His mouth goeth a sharp sword, that with it He should smite the nations: and He shall rule them with a rod of iron: and He treadeth the winepress of the fierceness and wrath of Almighty God."

2. It comes with amazing <u>SIGNS</u> in the heavens!

Joel 2:31 – "the sun shall be turned into darkness, and the moon into blood"

II Peter 3:10-12 – "But the day of the Lord will come as a thief in the night; in the which the heavens shall pass away with a great noise, and the elements shall melt with fervent heat, the earth also and the works that are therein shall be burned up. Seeing then that all these things shall be dissolved, what manner of persons ought ye to be in all holy conversation and godliness, Looking for and hasting unto the *coming of the day of God, wherein the heavens being on fire shall be dissolved, and the elements shall melt with fervent heat."*

These catastrophic events are a reminder to all of us that the coming DAY of the LORD will be unlike anything we have ever seen in previous history!

3. It comes in much <u>SORROW</u>!

Joel 2:11 – *"for the day of the Lord is great and very terrible; and who can abide it?"*

Zephaniah 1:14 – *"The great day of the LORD is near, it is near, and hasteth greatly, even the voice of the day of the LORD: the mighty man shall cry there bitterly."*

Revelation 6:15-17 – *"And the kings of the earth, and the great men, and the rich men, and the chief captains, and the mighty men, and every bondman, and every free man, hid themselves in the dens and in the rocks of the mountains; And said to the mountains and rocks, Fall on us, and hide us from the face of Him that sitteth on the throne, and from the wrath of the Lamb; For the great day of His wrath is come; and who shall be able to stand?"*

THE SEVERE <u>CONSEQUENCES</u> WILL COME UPON PEOPLE OTHER THAN BELIEVERS AT THAT TIME!

The pronouns in I Thessalonians 5:1-11 are extremely important to understand.

The word *"ye"* – vv. 1, 4, 5, 11
The word *"yourselves"* – vv. 2, 11
The word *"us"* – vv. 6, 8, 9, 10
The word *"we"* – vv. 5, 10
The word *"brethren"* – vv. 1, 4
The words *"one another"* – v. 11

The above words refer to believers only.

The word *"they"* – vv. 3, 7
The word *"them"* – v. 3
The word *"others"* – v. 6

These words refer to unbelievers only.

v. 3 – *"sudden destruction cometh upon <u>them</u>"* and *"<u>they</u> shall not escape"*

1. Unbelievers will be <u>HUMBLED!</u>

Isaiah 2:11-12 – *"The lofty looks of man shall be humbled, and the haughtiness of men shall be bowed down, and the LORD alone shall be exalted in that day. For the day of the LORD of hosts shall be upon every one that is proud and lofty, and upon every one that is lifted up; and he shall be brought low."*

Isaiah 2:17 – *"And the loftiness of man shall be bowed down, and the haughtiness of men shall be made low: and the LORD alone shall be exalted in that day."*

2. Unbelievers will be <u>DESTROYED!</u>

Isaiah 13:9 – *"Behold, the day of the LORD cometh, cruel both with wrath and fierce anger, to lay the land desolate: and He shall destroy the sinners thereof out of it."*

Jeremiah 46:10a – *"For this is the day of the LORD God of hosts, a day of vengeance, that He may avenge Him of His adversaries..."*

Obadiah 1:15 – *"For the day of the LORD is near upon all the heathen: as thou hast done, it shall be done unto thee: thy reward shall return upon thine own head."*

3. Believers will be <u>DELIVERED</u>!

Joel 2:31-32 – *"The sun shall be turned into darkness, and the moon into blood, before the great and the terrible day of the LORD come. And it shall come to pass, that whosoever shall call on the Name of the LORD shall be delivered: for in mount Zion and in Jerusalem shall be deliverance, as the LORD hath said, and in the remnant whom the LORD shall call."*

Acts 2:19-21 – *"And I will shew wonders in heaven above, and signs in the earth beneath; blood, and fire, and vapor of smoke: The sun shall be turned into darkness, and the moon into blood, before that great and notable day of the LORD come: And it shall come to pass, that whosoever shall call on the Name of the Lord shall be saved."*

THE <u>CONTRAST</u> BETWEEN THE LIGHT AND THE DARKNESS

I Thessalonians 5:4-5 – *"But ye, brethren, are not in darkness, that that day should overtake you as a thief. Ye are all the children of light, and the children of the day: we are not of the night nor of darkness."*

1. It is a <u>PROMISE</u> – *"not in darkness, that that day should overtake you as a thief"*

The word *"darkness"* is used 168 times, 51 of which are in the New Testament. The Hebrew prophets that deal with the coming of the DAY of the LORD use the word *"darkness"* 35 times. In the New Testament, the word is used in the following ways:

(1) It refers to *"outer darkness"* – hell itself!

Matthew 8:12 – *"But the children of the kingdom shall be cast out into outer darkness; there shall be weeping and gnashing of teeth."*

Matthew 22:13 – *"...cast him into outer darkness; there shall be weeping and gnashing of teeth."*

Matthew 25:30 – *"And cast ye the unprofitable servant into outer darkness: there shall be weeping and gnashing of teeth."*

      (2)   It refers to *"chains of darkness"*!

II Peter 2:4 – *"For if God spared not the angels that sinned, but cast them down to hell, and delivered them into chains of darkness, to be reserved unto judgment"*

      (3)   It is used of the *"power of darkness"*!

Luke 22:53 – *"When I was daily with you in the temple, ye stretched forth no hands against Me: but this is your hour, and the power of darkness."*

Colossians 1:13 – *"Who hath delivered us from the power of darkness, and hath translated us into the kingdom of His dear Son."*

      (4)   It refers to the *"works of darkness"*!

Romans 13:12 – *"The night is far spent, the day is at hand: let us therefore cast off the works of darkness, and let us put on the armor of light."*

Ephesians 5:11 – *"And have no fellowship with the unfruitful works of darkness, but rather reprove them."*

> **(5)** It refers to those who *"sit in darkness"*!

Luke 1:79 – *"To give light to them that sit in darkness and in the shadow of death, to guide our feet into the way of peace."*

> **(6)** It speaks of those who *"walk in darkness"*!

John 8:12 – *"I am the light of the world: he that followeth Me shall not walk in darkness, but shall have the light of life."*

I John 1:6 – *"If we say that we have fellowship with Him, and walk in darkness, we lie, and do not the truth."*

> **(7)** It refers to the coming *"day of the Lord"*!

Amos 5:18-20 – *"Woe unto you that desire the day of the LORD! to what end is to for you? the day of the LORD is darkness, and not light. As if a man did flee from a lion, and a bear met him; or went into the house, and leaned his hand on the wall, and a serpent bit him. Shall not the day of the LORD be darkness, and not light? Even very dark, and no brightness in it?"*

Zephaniah 1:15 – *"That day is a day of wrath, a day of trouble and distress, a day of wasteness and desolation, a day of darkness and gloominess, a day of clouds and thick darkness."*

2. It is a <u>POSITION</u> based upon our faith in the Lord Yeshua!

John 8:12 – *"I am the light of the world: he that followeth Me shall not walk in darkness, but shall have the light of life."*

John 12:35-36 – *"Yet a little while is the light with you. Walk while ye have the light, lest darkness come upon you: for he that walketh in darkness knoweth not whither he goeth. While ye have light, believe in the light, that ye may be the children of light."*

I John 1:6-7 – *"If we say that we have fellowship with Him, and walk in darkness, we lie, and do not the truth: But if we walk in the light, as He is in the light, we have fellowship one with another, and the blood of Jesus Christ His Son cleanseth us from all sin."*

3. It is a <u>PRACTICE!</u>

John 3:19-21 – *"And this is the condemnation, that light is come into the world, and men loved darkness rather than light, because their deeds were evil. For every one that doeth evil hateth the light, neither cometh to the light, lest his deeds should be reproved. But he that doeth truth cometh to the light, that his deeds be made manifest, that they are wrought in God."*

Ephesians 5:8-11 – *"For ye were sometimes darkness, but now are ye light in the Lord: walk as children of light: For the fruit of the Spirit is in all goodness and righteousness and truth; Proving what is acceptable unto the Lord. And have no fellowship with the unfruitful works of darkness, but rather reprove them."*

I John 2:9-11 – *"He that saith he is in the light, and hateth his brother, is in darkness even until now. He that loveth his brother abideth in the light, and there is none occasion of stumbling in him. But he that hateth his brother is in darkness, and walketh in darkness, and knoweth not whither he goeth, because that darkness hath blinded his eyes."*

Those who *"walk in the light"* are believers, and those who *"walk in the darkness"* are unbelievers. Believers, however, are challenged to not *"walk in darkness."*

THE <u>CHALLENGE</u> TO BELIEVERS BECAUSE OF THE CONTRAST BETWEEN LIGHT AND DARKNESS!

I Thessalonians 5:6-8 – *"Therefore let us not sleep, as do others; but let us watch and be sober. For they that sleep sleep in the night; and they that be drunken are drunken in the night. But let us, who are of the day, be sober, putting on the breastplate of faith and love; and for an helmet, the hope of salvation."*

Two times in this brief paragraph we are told to *"be sober."* The command to *"watch"* is frequent in the Bible, and for two reasons:

> **(1)** **Because of the <u>WEAKNESS</u> of the flesh!**

Matthew 26:41 – *"Watch and pray, that ye enter not into temptation: the spirit indeed is willing, but the flesh is weak."*

The Greek word for *"weak"* is *asthenes* which means "without ability or strength" – in other words, the flesh is totally helpless – we need the strength of the Lord!

> **(2)** **Because of the <u>WORK</u> of the devil!**

I Peter 5:8 – *"Be sober, be vigilant; because your adversary the devil, as a roaring lion, walketh about, seeking whom he may devour."*

We are told in I Thessalonians 5:8 that we need to put on spiritual armor. A parallel passage in Ephesians 6:13-17:

"Wherefore take unto you the whole armor of God, that ye may be able to withstand in the evil day, and having done all, to stand. Stand therefore, having you loins gift about with truth, and having on the breastplate of righteousness; and your feet shod with the preparation of the gospel of peace; Above all, taking the shield of faith, wherewith ye shall be able to quench all the fiery darts of the wicked (one). And take the helmet of salvation, and the sword of the Spirit, which is the word of God."

THE <u>CONFIDENCE</u> WE HAVE BECAUSE WE ARE CHILDREN OF LIGHT!

I Thessalonians 5:9-10 — *"For God hath not appointed us to wrath, but to obtain salvation by our Lord Jesus Christ, Who died for us, that, whether we wake or sleep, we should live together with Him."*

1. Our **APPOINTMENT** is not *"to wrath"*!

The *"wrath"* in the context of I Thessalonians 5 is the coming DAY of the LORD. Hell is certainly a place that results from the wrath of God against our sin and rebellion. But, this is not what I Thessalonians 5 is about – it is about the coming DAY of the LORD!

In I Thessalonians 1:10 we read: *"And to wait for His Son from heaven, Whom He raised from the dead, even Jesus, Which delivered us from the wrath to come."* Once again, this is a promise that brings the believer great confidence – we will not experience the coming wrath of the DAY of the LORD!

Revelation 3:10 is a message to the church of Philadelphia:

"Because thou hast kept the word of My patience, I also will keep thee from the hour of temptation, which shall come upon all the world, to try them that dwell on the earth."

WHAT A WONDERFUL PROMISE!

The phrase *"them that dwell upon the earth"* is used several times in the Book of Revelation and refers to unbelievers, NOT believers!

Also, the words *"the hour of temptation"* are not referring to general temptation that believers face (cf. I Corinthians 10:13). The definite article in Greek stands in front of the word *"hour"* and in front of the word *"temptation."* It is referring to "<u>THE</u> hour of <u>THE</u> temptation" – it is speaking of the specific trial that comes to the whole world. The words *"which shall come upon all the world"* clarify that it is speaking about the coming tribulation or the coming DAY of the LORD.

Some teach that this is simply a promise of immunity from the judgments of the tribulation. However, there will be many who become believers during the tribulation who will, in fact, be martyred for their faith in the Lord and their refusal to take the mark of the beast or to worship his image.

The text says that the Lord will *"keep thee from"* this coming holocaust of judgment from the wrath of God. The

Greek preposition is *ek* meaning "out of" – it is not speaking of immunity, but rather of REMOVAL!

    2. Our <u>ASSURANCE</u> is based on the work of salvation!

All believers who have been born again (whether Jewish or Gentile) during this present time will be removed BEFORE the DAY of the LORD comes! Praise the Lord!

THE <u>COMFORT</u> WE HAVE BECAUSE WE ARE CHILDREN OF LIGHT!

I Thessalonians 5:11 – *"Wherefore comfort yourselves together, and edify one another, even as also ye do."*

Two things should characterize our relationships as believers with one another in the light of the Rapture (I Thessalonians 4:13-18) and the promise of being rescued from the coming wrath of God:

    1. We should constantly <u>ENCOURAGE</u> one another!

The Greek word *parakaleite* that is translated as *"comfort"* refers to a person who is "called alongside of" another in order to encourage that person.

Hebrews 10:24-25 – *"And let us consider one another to provoke unto love and to good works: Not forsaking the assembling of ourselves together, as the manner of some is; but exhorting one another; and so much the more, as ye see the day approaching."*

   2. We should constantly <u>EDIFY</u> one another!

The Greek word *oikodomeite* which is translated by the English word *"edify"* means "to build up" – it is the opposite of being critical and tearing a person down. Ephesians 4:16 says that this kind of *"edifying"* occurs in the sphere and arena of *"love."* I Corinthians 8:1 tells us that it is God's love that edifies or builds people up!

A FINAL WORD!

In this same chapter of I Thessalonians 5, we have some wonderful admonitions presented in verses 14-28 – take time to read them carefully!

I Thessalonians 5:14-28

"Now we exhort you, brethren, warn them that are unruly, comfort the feebleminded, support the weak, be patient toward all men. See that none render evil for evil unto any man; but ever follow that which is good, both among yourselves, and to all men. Rejoice evermore. Pray without ceasing. In every thing give thanks: for this is the will of God in Christ Jesus concerning you. Quench not the Spirit. Despise not prophesyings. Prove all things; hold fast that which is good. Abstain from all appearance of evil. And the very God of peace sanctify you wholly; and I pray your whole spirit and soul and body be preserved blameless unto the coming of our Lord Jesus Christ. Faithful is He that calleth you, Who also will do it. Brethren, pray for us. Greet all the brethren with an holy kiss. I charge you by the Lord that this epistle be read unto all the holy brethren. The grace of our Lord Jesus Christ be with you. AMEN!"

Here is a list of what believers should be doing in the light of the LORD's return!

WARN the unruly!
COMFORT the feebleminded!
SUPPORT the weak!
BE PATIENT toward all!
FORGIVE those who hurt you!
FOLLOW the good!
REJOICE always!
PRAY without ceasing!
GIVE THANKS for everything!
QUENCH NOT the Holy Spirit!
DESPISE NOT the proclaiming of truth!
PROVE all things!
HOLD FAST to the good!
ABSTAIN from the appearance of evil!
PRAY for God's servants!
GREET all believers with a holy kiss!

Yes, we are exhorted to do all the above things! The DAY of the LORD is coming – the Bible is filled with that powerful message!

There is no more important issue in life that making sure of our relationship to the LORD – our blessed Lord Yeshua, the Messiah of Israel and our Redeemer!

Steve Linde
713 N 6th St
98982